LIZ EARLE'S
QUICK GUIDES
Vegetarian Cookery

GW00601097

For Lily, Guy and all animal lovers.

LIZ EARLE'S
QUICK GUIDES
Vegetarian Cookery

BOXTREE

First published in Great Britain in 1994 by Boxtree Limited,
Broadwall House, 21 Broadwall, London SE1 9PL

10 9 8 7 6 5 4 3 2 1

ISBN: 1 85283 546 X

Text design by Blackjacks
Cover design by Hammond Hammond

Printed and Bound in Great Britain by Cox & Wyman Ltd.,
Reading, Berkshire

A CIP catalogue entry for this book is available from
the British Library

Contents

ACKNOWLEDGEMENTS

I am grateful to Sarah Mobsby for helping to produce this book. Also to the cookery schools, whose vegetarian cooking courses I have attended for fun as well as epicurean research. In particular, Leith's School of Food and Wine, Westminster Catering College and the Ballymaloe Cookery School. I am also indebted to the talented team at Boxtree, Rosemary Sandberg and Claire Bowles, Publicity, for their unfailing enthusiasm and support.

Introduction

There are so many very good reasons for cooking vegetarian that they are too numerous to list in this simple *Quick Guide*. However, I hope this small book will give you an insight into the many health advantages as well as the taste benefits of this 'green' cuisine. Although I applaud all steps taken to end unnecessary animal suffering, at the same time, all vegetarians and the even stricter vegans, need to ensure that they obtain their full quota of vital vitamins and other nutrients. This is why I have included a separate chapter on the importance of vegetarian nutrition. Last, but by no means least, modern vegetarian food is so delicious that no one need ever ask 'but where's the meat?' I have included many of my own family's personal favourite recipes which I hope you also enjoy sharing with your family and friends.

Liz Earle

—1—
Why Cook Vegetarian?

Over the past few years we have been bombarded by the arguments for and against vegetarianism. From a purely physical point of view, human beings are omnivores, which means that we have the choice of whether to eat meat or not as opposed to herbivores who cannot eat meat and carnivores who have to eat meat to survive. However, there are many valid reasons why we should definitely cut down on our meat eating, if not give it up altogether.

Here's to your health

Appealing to your instincts of self-preservation, it is a fact of life that, over all, vegetarians are healthier. This is because a vegetarian diet naturally pulls you along the road of healthy eating. Plenty of complex carbohydrates (grains, potatoes and pulses) form a solid base. Piled on top are added vital vitamins and minerals from all those fresh fruit and vegetables. Combine this with a greatly reduced saturated fat intake from eating no meat and the end result is a healthier diet and therefore a healthier body. Of course it is possible to be vegetarian and have a terrible diet, but the healthy way is better signposted. There is also a pleasant surprise in store as once you get used to a better diet, you will no longer like the thought of fatty, heavy and high-calorie foods.

Many people are scared of not getting enough protein in their diet if they become vegetarians. But entire cultures have thrived for thousands of years on virtually vegetarian diets. In fact, it is argued that naturally man eats predominantly plant matter, with animals as an occasional item. Our digestive tract is long and winding, whereas in those animals which are meant to eat a lot of meat, it is much shorter. This indicates that we were not designed to consume vast amounts of animal products. This balance of low animal and high plant foods is still found in primitive cultures and tribes, and also in some of the healthiest nations in the world. It is very difficult for anyone who has enough to eat to be deficient in protein – eating a balanced diet incorporating dairy produce, grains, pulses, nuts and seeds provides plentiful protein.

With today's factory farming and high-tech agrochemical methods of rearing, meat may harm our bodies with a multiplicity of toxins. There are several reasons for this. As meat is further up the food chain than plant matter, substances such as pesticides and fertilisers are found in a far more concentrated form in animal meat. Also, farmed animals' diets sometimes contain weird and unnatural things, such as sheep's brains and fish gristle. In addition, there is the use of synthetic growth hormones and genetic engineering – we do not yet know the full consequences of altering the path of nature. However, we do know that the results can be dangerous, witness the unfortunate evidence of BSE, better known as Mad Cow Disease.

The wealth of the world

It has been put to us that the world is capable of feeding all the people in it. But how can this be so when there are starving masses in the Third World? Many of those people are starving as a direct consequence of the greed of western nations. For many farmers it is more profitable to grow cash crops, to feed to animals, to feed the rich. This is in preference to selling their crops to the local people who simply wish to eat. If we take one acre of land and grow soya beans, there would be enough to feed a man for five years. However, if on the same piece of land we grow barley to rear beef cattle, the end result would feed a man for only four months. So we have on our hands a selfish and wasteful system. This is continually fuelled by multinational self-interest to the detriment of the poor of the world. The only way we can stop this chain of events is to make it unprofitable – and the only real power we have to do that is with our money. Spend yours wisely.

Cruelty-free foods

Imagine being in a space which is too small for you to turn around in, or even full lift your head up. Underneath you is a harsh metal grating, the only surface for you to stand on, or lie down to try to get some sleep. Your excrement and urine falls on to (and hopefully through) this same grating. The air is smelly and dank. You are fed an unnatural diet. Treated with hormones, you grow abnormally fast and your young, unexercised legs cannot cope. Your existence is full of pain. Perhaps among the worst of the deprivations is that you are allowed no interaction with your fellow beings. Then your short and miserable life comes to its conclusion, you may be given only a few seconds of electric stunning (as opposed to the legal requirement of eight) meaning you are still conscious as your throat is slit.

This type of existence is not uncommon for many factory-farmed animals. If your reaction is that they are only animals, I would ask you to think of creatures in more natural habitats. Most of the animals that are commonly farmed are clean, active and sociable when in the wild.

For those who really cannot bear to give up meat altogether, I would advise you first of all to cut down on meat to gain all the health benefits. Then, with the money saved, buy the so-called 'kind meats'. That means paying extra and buying organic meats. Add to this other 'kinder' foods such as game birds, free-living fish and shellfish and you have a wide range of tastes at your disposal. All these animals live in humane conditions not too unlike their natural habitat. You may well be further surprised, as the meat from these sources is tastier than the bland stuff filling most of the supermarket shelves. It will also contain a far lower proportion of saturated fat, as an active, moving animal is of necessity leaner than the stationary one. Buying 'kinder' products also applies to strict vegetarians. Free-range eggs and organic milk are now widely available. Factory farming of eggs creates among the cruellest conditions to be found. Milk production can also lead to a miserable life for the cow and often even worse fates for the calves. The sooner we show we want to buy the products of cruelty-free and organic farming, the sooner some of these horrific practices will die out. So once more I urge you to put the power of the consumer to good use.

Eat for enjoyment

Vegetarian cookery is now a cuisine in its own right. Gone are the days of dry, boring, tasteless vegetarian food with a sprinkling of nuts or lentils on everything. Now vegetarian fare is gourmet food with a full spectrum of tastes and textures. Imaginative cooking has taken inspiration from cultures the world over. Strangely enough, it is now the 'meat and two veg' eaters who are missing out on the best taste sensations.

This all adds up to a very convincing argument for turning your back on meat eating. So start cooking food which pleases the palate and the eye and can be eaten with peace of mind and a clear conscience.

—— 2 ——
Vegetarian Nutrition

You are what you eat! It is therefore of utmost importance to understand the basics of nutrition. The big building blocks for the body are the macronutrients – proteins, carbohydrates and fats. Equally necessary are the tiny blocks of the micronutrients – vitamins and minerals. More important for life than food is water, as a human can last for quite a while without food but for only a few days without water. These six are the essentials for a healthy life.

The Macronutrients

PROTEIN

Proteins are fundamental to all living matter. In humans, protein accounts for 17 percent of our total body mass. Proteins are used for the growth and repair of our bodies, being required for these purposes by each individual cell. Their second function is to maintain supplies of enzymes, hormones and antibodies. Any excess can be stored and used later as a source of energy.

Proteins are made up of amino acids, of which there are over twenty. The body needs all of these, but can synthesise some of them itself. There are eight amino acids which are termed 'essential' as the body cannot make them and so needs to acquire a supply of them through the diet. The eight essentials are:

- ***** isoleucine
- ***** leucine
- ***** lysine
- ***** methionine
- ***** phenylalanine
- ***** threonine
- ***** tryptophan
- ***** valine

Proteins from animal sources, such as milk and eggs, contain all of these in approximately the proportions the body needs, and are hence called 'complete' proteins. However, vegetarians should not rely on dairy products for their entire protein intake, but make use of other sources. At this point it is worth mentioning the soya bean which is a non-animal food that contains the eight essential amino acids. Therefore, soya beans and soya bean products are particularly important for vegetarians. It is important to remember that other non-animal sources, such as legumes (other than soya beans) and grains, are 'incomplete' proteins. This means that they do not contain all the essential amino acids and need to be properly combined.

To make complete protein from incomplete proteins eat:
- ***** Legumes with grains/nuts and seeds.
- ***** Grains with legumes.
- ***** Nuts and seeds with legumes.

This is actually easy to do as many common dishes combine these naturally: baked beans on toast; lentil lasagne; pea soup with bread; pizza and peas; houmous (combines chick peas and sesame seeds); bean and nut salads; lentil bake with sesame seeds and almonds ... the list is endless and the only boundary is your imagination.

CARBOHYDRATE

Carbohydrates are made up of carbon, hydrogen and oxygen and they are manufactured by plants through the process of photosynthesis. This is when the plant makes starch using the energy from sunlight. Carbohydrates form a large part of our diet and are an important source of energy.

There is a whole spectrum of differently sized molecules within carbohydrates. The size of molecule provides a rough guide to the value of that type of carbohydrate in terms of nutrition – the larger the molecule the better the carbohydrate is for us. This is because the larger molecules are found in the complex carbohydrates, which release their energy gradually. Complex carbohydrates are foods such as potatoes, pasta, grains and bread which should make up the majority of our diet. The smaller molecules are the sugars which release their energy very swiftly into the blood. While this can provide a pick-me-up, it is very short-lived and is rapidly followed by a sugar low, which makes us feel tired, lethargic and can even cause headaches. This sugar 'low' also creates a craving for more sugar, which if indulged can result in a sugar cycle of cravings, energy bursts and depressing lows. This leads to many health problems and weight-gain.

When talking about sugar, it is important to draw a distinction between extrinsic and intrinsic sugar. Intrinsic sugar is that naturally found in a food, such as the fructose found in fruit and the lactose found in milk, whereas extrinsic sugar is that which is added to food. This is the sugar which is bad for us and is also totally unnecessary. If you do have a sugar craving, try to satisfy it with some fruit – white grapes are especially good being a particularly sweet fruit and handy to nibble. The advantage of the intrinsic sugar, fructose, in the fruit is that it does not mean 'empty calories' as you are also getting a healthy dose of vitamins and dietary fibre. You are also unlikely to eat anywhere near the same amount of sugar; it would take twenty large, sweet apples to provide the same amount of sugar as 100g (4oz) refined sugar. Other ways to cut down on refined, extrinsic sugar include buying sugar-free breakfast cereals, drinking juices as opposed to commercial sugary drinks, replacing desserts with fruit and yoghurts and as a rule of thumb when following a recipe – halve the amount of sugar used.

The largest size of carbohydrate molecule is found in cellulose, which is indigestible and is more commonly known as dietary fibre. Although this does not provide nutrition as it cannot be absorbed, it is essential for our digestive systems to operate effectively and healthily. A diet high in dietary fibre seems to reduce the risk of diabetes, cancer of the bowel and heart disease. It also helps prevent constipation, combat weight gain and absorb some toxic chemicals. Again in this area vegetarians score well, as most eat a diet high in fibre. But to increase your fibre intake avoid refined foods, eat plenty of wholegrains, legumes and vegetables.

The other vitally important point to be made about carbohydrates is the distinction between refined and unrefined carbohydrates. The unrefined and more natural forms are definitely the healthier alternatives. The refined forms have often been stripped of most, if not all, of their vitamins, minerals and a large proportion of dietary fibre. For instance white flour has lost up to 80 percent of its vitamins and nutrients through processing. It is very easy to make the change from refined to unrefined versions and this simple switch can vastly improve anyone's diet, with very little effort.

Table 1
Refined versus unrefined foods

REFINED = LESS HEALTHY	UNREFINED = MORE HEALTHY

Sugars:
    Sugar (including anything made with sugar, eg biscuits, cakes, jellies, soft drinks, etc)
    Sweets
    Honey
	Sugars:
	    Fruit
	    Vegetables
	    Juices (fruit/vegetable)
	    Puddings and biscuits, etc made with the sugars found in fruit

Complex carbohydrates:
    White flour, bread and pasta
    White rice
    Processed breakfast cereals (although some are better than others)
	Complex carbohydrates:
	    Brown flour, bread and pasta
	    Brown rice (brown is beautiful!)
	    Whole-grain breakfast cereals
	    Potatoes
	    Pulses

FATS

Fat is a necessary component of our bodies. Fat keeps us warm, is a store of energy, keeps our skin and arteries supple, protects our internal organs and is essential for proper brain function. In a normal man it accounts for about 12 percent of the total body weight and in a woman about 25 percent.

But fat has had a very bad press in recent years. This is slightly misleading as we do actually need to eat some fat.

However, most of us eat too much fat and often fat of the wrong sort. It is recommended that we get no more than a maximum 30 percent of all our calories from fat, while the average intake is around 45 percent. More significant is the *type* of fat we eat. There are two main types – saturated and unsaturated.

Saturated fats are only really useful as a source of energy and padding, and could lead to harmful high cholesterol levels and the possibility of coronary disease later in life. As adults we obtain enough energy from other sources so it is totally unnecessary to eat saturated fat – so cut saturated fat out of your diet as much as possible. This baddie is found in animal and dairy products. It is very simple to cut down the amount of saturated fat by switching to skimmed or semi-skimmed milk, always cooking with vegetable oils instead of butter and using yoghurt or smetana in recipes in place of cream. On average a third of a British person's fat intake comes from meat and another third from dairy products. Therefore, vegetarians will already be eating less fat than average and this is one of the reasons vegetarians are statistically far healthier.

Unsaturated fats on the other hand are derived from vegetable sources. These fats are generally liquid at room temperature, and so are called oils. Chemically speaking an oil is exactly the same as a fat. As well as providing the all-important essential fatty acids, dietary fats are often carriers of the fat-soluble vitamins A, D, E and K. Use a vegetable oil such as olive oil when cooking in place of butter or other saturated fats. When buying your vegetable oils make sure you buy cold-pressed, unrefined oils as these contain the highest levels of nutrients (refined versions look paler as they have been largely stripped of their nutrients).

The Micronutrients

VITAMINS
Vitamins are essential for complete health. The human body is unable to manufacture them (with the exception of vitamin D produced in the skin in the presence of sunlight) so they must

Table 2
Vitamins

VITAMIN	NEEDED FOR	GOOD SOURCES
Fat soluble:		
A	growth, healthy skin, lungs, good night vision	orange/red/dark green fruit and vegetables (eg carrots, tomatoes, sweet potatoes, apricots, peaches, broccoli, watercress), eggs, buttermilk, (beta-carotene is a form of vitamin A which acts as an antioxidant destroying free radicals, and this is found in colourful fruit and vegetables.)
D	bone formation and health (it works in conjunction with calcium)	eggs, butter, vegetable oils; the majority of our require ments are fulfilled by the vitamin D produced by the skin in the presence of sunlight.

VITAMIN	NEEDED FOR	GOOD SOURCES
E	maintaining healthy cell structure, good circulation and maintaining red blood cells; an antioxidant	vegetable oils, nuts, seeds, wholegrains, avocados
K	blood clotting and bone maintenance	present in our intestines, found in most vegetables and wholegrain cereals

Water soluble:

VITAMIN	NEEDED FOR	GOOD SOURCES
C	strengthening the immune system, helping fight infection, aiding growth of healthy tissue; an antioxidant	fruit (especially citrus fruits, melons, strawberries and tomatoes), vegetables (especially potatoes, broccoli, spinach and cauliflower)
B complex (there are many B vitamins)	growth, healthy nervous system, aid to digestion converting food into energy, healthy skin, eyes mouth and liver, red blood cell formation	yeast extract, dairy produce, whole-grain cereals, nuts, dark green vegetables
B2 & B12	Of the B complex vitamins, vegetarians have to be especially careful to ensure they are getting sufficient B2 and B12 from their diets.	B2 – yeast extract, wheat-germ, dairy products including eggs, soya flour, green leafy vegetables, pulses B12 – eggs, cheese, yoghurt, milk and miso yeast extract

be obtained through the food we eat. Diets lacking in particular vitamins may produce vitamin deficiency diseases, including scurvy, beriberi and rickets. However, they are not needed simply to prevent these diseases but also for the efficient day-to-day running of the complex machine of the human body. Recent research has begun to show that vitamins have an amazing impact on our health. However, many of us do not receive the levels of vitamins necessary for this optimum nutrition, especially with the destruction of vitamins through storage and food-processing methods and the increased needs of our bodies caused by today's pollution and stressful living. It is therefore recommended that most adults take a good multivitamin supplement.

In the vitamin table (see pages 16–17), the nutrients have been divided into fat or water soluble vitamins. The body is able to store the fat soluble vitamins; so as long as the body receives enough it can regulate its own supply and demand. The body is unable to store the water soluble vitamins, what is not needed there and then is excreted from the body in urine. Therefore, it is necessary to keep the supply of these vitamins fairly constant to avoid running short.

MINERALS

Around 6 percent of our body weight is made up of minerals. Calcium, phosphorus and magnesium are the principal constituents of our bones. Vegans have to be careful to obtain enough calcium in their diet, as they eat no dairy products. The other minerals which are essential for us to live are used to regulate and balance our body chemistry. Iron deficiency is the most prevalent single nutrient deficiency in the world, affecting one billion people – one-fifth of the world's population. Iron is also a mineral often lacking in vegetarian diets, as meat is most people's main source. So it is important to think about incorporating foods rich in iron into the diet and maybe buying iron-fortified foods.

Table 3
Minerals

MINERAL	NEEDED FOR	GOOD SOURCES
Calcium	strong, healthy bones (especially in childhood), good teeth, efficient muscle working	dairy produce, especially milk, broccoli, spinach, watercress, dried figs, pulses, almonds
Iron	healthy blood (iron is a vital component of haemoglobin which transports oxygen around the body) and muscles	egg yolks, dried fruits (especially apricots), wholegrains, pulses green vegetables
Magnesium	healthy bones and muscles (works with calcium), protein and hormone organisation	green leafy vegetables, nuts, seeds
Potassium	nerve transmission, water balance	fruit, vegetables, wholegrains
Sodium	nerve transmission, water balance	salt – but we do not need to add any extra sodium (salt) as it is present in most foods in small amounts

Chromium, copper, manganese, selenium and zinc are known as the 'trace' minerals. They are all essential for us to remain healthy but we only require them in tiny amounts.

WATER

The spring of life – water is essential for us all to live. About 60 percent of the human body is made up of water. We lose water through urine, the skin and the lungs. This water is replaced through drinking and eating. A rough guide to when we need more water is the feeling of thirst, but by the time you feel thirsty your body has been dehydrated for around twenty minutes. So it is important to drink fluids even when you do not feel thirsty.

The Young Vegetarian

Children and teenagers are the fastest expanding group of vegetarians. Some are brought up as vegetarians, but many teenagers make the decision themselves and this must be applauded. However, a good diet is particularly important for growing bodies. While it is easier to monitor the diets of younger children, at least for two meals a day, this is nigh on impossible for teenagers. Unfortunately, this is the group of the population with the worst diet in nutritional terms. The problem is compounded in the case of teenage girls who diet heavily and can become anaemic. So it is wise to suggest a good multivitamin and mineral supplement with iron. Older children and teenagers love quick, easy food which they can get for themselves – keep the fridge stocked with ready-to-eat (healthy, of course) snacks. More generally, try to ensure or encourage a good balanced diet, which is relatively easy in smaller children. Try to encourage fruit, or a sandwich for a snack or, if they can't be weaned off sweet things, make puddings with lots of fruit

(and therefore natural sugars). Calcium is particularly important for growing bodies. Try to encourage drinking milk regularly (semi-skimmed or skimmed once over three years' old) as
a refreshing cold drink or with lunch. All kids love the taste
sensation of a home-made milk shake.

The Baddies

The six dietary sins:

* salt
* saturated fat
* sugar
* chemical additives
* alcohol
* caffeine

SALT

At present the average adult daily intake is 12g daily, whereas
the World Health Organisation recommends no more than 5g
daily. In actual fact salt is only necessary in the tiny quantities
that one easily obtains naturally from foods without adding any
extra. An excess of salt puts strain on the kidneys, and may be a
contributory factor in high blood pressure. The easiest way to
cut down is to avoid processed foods containing salt, as many
are loaded with it – quite unnecessarily. Salt is included in many
surprising foods such as breakfast cereals and canned vegetables, as well as the more obvious crisps, butter and pickles. The
other golden rules are never to add it when cooking (herbs and
spices give foods plenty of flavour) and not to have a salt cellar
on the table.

SATURATED FAT

Our diet as a nation contains far too much saturated fat, but this
was not always so. It is estimated that two centuries ago fat only

accounted for about 10 percent of the calories in the diet; now it makes up about 40 percent. Originally fatty foods could only be afforded by the richest, whereas now they are the cheapest form of calories available. Eating an excess is one of the main causes of our biggest killer – heart disease. It also leads to an increased risk of cancer. In the shorter term it means we put on weight and our lymphatic system slows down. We can cut out saturated fats with relative ease and replace them with unsaturated fats. See fats on pages 14–15.

SUGAR

Too much sugar makes us put on weight, which leads to high blood pressure, strokes and heart disease. An excess has also been linked to lowered immunity, kidney disorders, diabetes and some skin disorders. There is an unequivocal link between sugar and tooth decay. Most of us are aware of these horrifying consequences, yet each person on average in the Western world eats an average of 1kg (2lb) every week. The problem lies with refined sugars which are totally unnecessary (see pages 12–14).

CHEMICAL ADDITIVES

Added to many processed foods to give them the 'right' taste, texture and colour. Although substances have always been added to foods to preserve them and make them appetising, the amount added to today's processed foods is on a totally different scale. They are preservatives, stabilisers, emulsifiers, colourings, flavour enhancers and artificial sweeteners. Many of the common additives are known to cause allergic reactions and hyperactivity in some people. Some can also have longer term effects on our health, being harmful over a prolonged exposure, a few for instance are thought to be carcinogenic. The idea of walking into a laboratory and eating and drinking the contents of all those glass containers is not appealing, and yet that is effectively what you do when you eat some processed foods.

The message is, where possible cook your own foods from whole natural ingredients, preferably using organic produce. When buying processed foods, get into the habit of reading the labels to avoid any nasty substances. As a quick rule of thumb, if you do not recognise any of the ingredients as foodstuffs because they are chemical names, do not buy the product.

ALCOHOL

Here the maxim 'everything in moderation' is the essential rule. A little alcohol is not bad, as it relaxes and so can release tension and stress. However, too much alcohol is bad (leaving aside the stupid things people do when drunk) as it damages the body. It causes dehydration, puts a huge strain on the liver, exhausts supplies of B vitamins and vitamin C and is even thought to kill off brain cells. Alcohol offers only empty calories, which in serious drinkers can be a real problem, meaning they do not get enough nutrients. It is recommended that men drink no more than 21 units and women no more than 14 units of alcohol a week. (One unit = half a pint of pint of beer, one 125ml glass of wine or one single measure of spirits.)

CAFFEINE

Caffeine is a stimulant found in coffee, tea, cola drinks and cocoa. As such it makes you feel more alert, but makes your heart beat more rapidly and irregularly. Too much induces sleeplessness and anxiety, raises the blood pressure and lowers blood sugar. It is thought that caffeine could inhibit the absorption of some vitamins and minerals. Caffeine can also trigger migraines in sensitive people. Much of the human population is addicted to caffeine, yet it is totally unnecessary. If you have to rely on a stimulant such as caffeine to get you through the day, your body is trying to tell you something. So take my advice and get a couple of early nights!

3
Vegetarian Food Finder

Grains

BARLEY
Barley comes from the Middle East but travelled west and has been cultivated in Europe for the last 2,000 years.

Pearl barley – These are the smooth, polished barley kernels which have been stripped of their fibrous husk. Although its fibre content is therefore reduced, it retains some nutrients and is excellent for thickening soups and stews.

Pot barley – The unrefined grain with its coating of nutritious barley bran has high levels of iron, calcium, potassium and B vitamins (notably folic acid) and it has unusually soothing properties on the stomach, digestive and urinary tracts. Soak overnight before using, but keep the soaking water for cooking as it will contain important vitamins. It takes about an hour to cook and is a delicious addition to rice dishes.

BUCKWHEAT
Historically, buckwheat has been important in times of famine as it grows from seed to kernel in a little over two months and thrives in the poorest soils. Originally grown in the Far East, buckwheat is a favourite food of the healthy and long-lived Buddhist monks. Despite its name, buckwheat is totally gluten-free and nothing like our common wheat. It contains B vitamins, potassium, magnesium and iron and is an excellent low-fat, non-animal source of complete protein so a very important food for vegetarians.

Buckwheat groats: Wash and cook in the same way as rice, using only the amount of water to be absorbed during cooking as the vitamins dissolve easily in water.

Buckwheat flour: A pale grey, speckled flour famous for making the gourmet pancakes or blinis served in traditional Russian cookery. Use buckwheat flour for baking and to thicken soups and sauces.

MAIZE

Maize or sweetcorn has been cultivated in America for thousands of years and can be traced back to Aztec civilisations. It was brought back to Britain from America by Christopher Columbus in 1492. A versatile, gluten-free grain that can be popped into popcorn for that video night at home.

Cornflour: Excellent gluten-free thickener for sauces and desserts.

Polenta: Ground maize or cornmeal is served on the Continent as a side dish or used to make dumplings and porridge. American cornmeal is much finer and goes into cornbread and muffins.

MILLET

Millet was once the most important cereal crop in Europe. Millet contains complete protein, more iron than other cereals and is a useful source of calcium and is also gluten-free. Cook as an alternative to rice, but 'crack' the tiny seeds first by frying them in a little olive oil to help them absorb enough cooking water.

OATS

Native to Scotland, oats are an important ingredient in many traditional Scottish dishes such as oatcakes and haggis. They contain protein, vitamins B and E, calcium and other minerals such as potassium and magnesium, as well as the healthy polyunsaturated fats. It is milled to a variety of textures for cooking and to make porridge. Oat bran contains an unusual fibre that reduces cholesterol and helps regulate blood sugar levels.

QUINOA

Quinoa (pronounced keenowa) is a tiny, golden grain similar in shape and texture to millet. Unlike most grains, quinoa does not belong to the grass family but is a relative of the garden weed commonly known as 'fat hen'. It has a higher protein content than most grains and is a source of essential fatty acids. Quinoa cooks quickly in 10-15 minutes and can be mixed with other grains to improve a fairly bland flavour.

RICE

Rice is a fabulous staple food for families all round the world. Provided it is stored in a cool, dry place rice will last almost indefinitely, so you can safely store several different types to use over a period of many months. There are over 7,000 varieties of rice, and it is inexpensive and easily available in many forms, including organically grown. All types of rice are easily digested and highly unlikely to cause any allergy problems, being gluten-free.

Basmati rice: This is a fine, long-grain rice from the foothills of the Himalayas. The aromatic flavour is the perfect accompaniment to curries or spicy foods. Look for brown basmati with more fibre and protein.

Brown rice: The whole rice pellet including its protective bran coating is an excellent source of fibre and protein. Brown rice also contains iron, calcium, B vitamins and many essential amino acids, and you wouldn't go far wrong if you ate it every day.

Cavolina or patna rice: Bland, with a papery taste, this is the rice most commonly found in packets. Generally highly polished it has lost most of its nutritional value.

Glutinous rice: Despite its name, it contains no gluten, but does have a sticky, glutinous texture making it easier to eat with chopsticks. Naturally sweet, it is a good choice for puddings.

Italian rice: The perfect choice for making risotto as its large, oval shape gives texture to those famous Italian rice dishes. The brown variety is both healthier and tastier.

Pudding rice: Highly polished, it gives little in the way of fibre. Sweet brown rice is a better choice for making puddings.

Rice flour: Flour is milled from both white and brown rice grains. A versatile cooking ingredient and can be used alone or mixed with other flours to make cakes and biscuits, or used to thicken soups, stews and sauces.

Sweet brown rice: The ultimate choice for rice pudding, sweet and sticky yet decidedly good for us.

Wild rice: Strictly speaking, wild rice is not a rice at all but a seed from an American water grass. Dark brown with a long, elegant shape and a uniquely nutty flavour, adding a spoonful to other rices turns an ordinary dish into something special.

RYE

Similar in composition to wheat but with a low gluten content. Black rye bread is a delicious alternative to your usual loaf and toasts well. Rye crispbread and crackers are also available.

SAGO

Easily digested, with no allergy problems, it is traditionally used for making milk puddings for invalids. Although bland and lacking in fibre, sago is useful for those on a restricted or gluten-free diet.

TAPIOCA

Tapioca is a small pellet made from manioc flour which comes from a tropical plant in Central Asia. Use as a gluten-free thickener or in milk puddings.

WHEAT

Wheat is Britain's most important crop and, not surprisingly, our diet is dominated by it. Over 30,000 varieties are said to be in cultivation but almost all belong to two main groups, one of which is used for bread making (it is the gluten which gives a loaf its elasticity) and the other of which is a harder wheat used in pasta and semolina. Wheat, and all its products, have a high gluten content.

Couscous: This is a refined wheat product made from semolina (see below) and is the staple food in North Africa. It is wonderfully easy to cook, but some of the wheat's original goodness is lost in processing and it lacks fibre.

Cracked wheat: Also known as bulgar wheat, this is a popular Middle Eastern wheat which has been cracked by boiling, then redried. Eat presoaked with salad for a nutritious snack.

Pasta: The great Italian invention made from wheat flours. Pasta comes in all shapes and sizes. Look for fresh pasta as a treat and also for the coloured varieties containing spinach and tomato.

Seitan: Seitan is a chewy, high protein food which can be bought as pastes or spreads. It is made from protein-rich wheat gluten. Cook in chunks or grate and use as meat eaters would use minced meat.

Semolina: This is the grittiest part of durum wheat which is sifted out. Semolina is a highly refined product and contains little fibre.

Wholewheat: The wholewheat kernel is the most nutritious way to enjoy wheat. Eat as you would rice, or soak and add to home-made bread or scones, soups and casseroles. Wholewheat is also superb sprouted.

Wheatgerm: This is the inner core of the wheat grain and is nature's richest source of vitamin E, high in protein and full of iron. Sprinkle a spoonful into soups, sauces, breakfast cereals and even desserts such as stewed apples or low-fat yoghurt.

Wholemeal flour: Bread, biscuits and cakes made with wholemeal flour (ground from wholewheat) contain more than twice as much fibre and other nutrients as those with white flour, so it is well worth making the switch.

Pulses and Beans

ADUKI BEANS

Aduki beans are valued in the Far East for their medicinal properties. Both the black and red varieties have an unusually sweet, quite strong flavour. Excellent in rice dishes and soups, or sprouted in salads and stir-frys.

BLACK-EYED BEANS

The slightly nutty flavour of these little beans often appeals to children. Black-eyed beans only need about forty minutes' cooking and do not require any soaking, so are good for that meal you are producing in a rush.

BORLOTTI BEANS

These Italian beans cook to a lovely creamy texture. Use instead of red kidney beans in dishes such as chillies, salads and soups.

BROAD BEANS

Broad beans were cultivated by the ancient Greeks and Egyptians. Although we are perhaps more familiar with fresh broad beans in this country, the dried beans have an earthy flavour particularly suited to stews.

BUTTER OR LIMA BEANS

Also known as Madagascar beans, these kidney-shaped beans retain their shape well when cooked. They have a mealy texture which absorbs other flavours well.

CHICK PEAS

There are several varieties of chick peas, available whole or split. Their savoury flavour gives houmous its distinctive taste. Chick peas ground into gram flour are excellent in savoury dishes.

DRIED PEAS

Often called blue peas, although tasty they have a floury texture, but are excellent in stews, soups and of course for the traditional mushy peas.

FLAGEOLET BEANS

This smaller relative of the haricot bean is very popular in France. The fresh flavour and green colour make flageolet beans particularly suitable for serving as a vegetable or in salads.

HARICOT BEANS

These are the beans which make the popular baked beans. Versatile with a good filling texture, they absorb flavours well.

LENTILS

The many varieties of lentils are commonly identified by their colour and are all rich in iron. An important ingredient in Indian cooking, they form the basis of dhal. Use green lentils as a good source of protein.

MUNG BEANS

Mung beans are probably better known in their sprouted form of beansprouts. The beans are small, round and normally green. With their high vitamin content they are an excellent bean to start incorporating in your diet.

RED KIDNEY BEANS

These handsome beans are particularly associated with Mexican cooking and spicy dishes. These quite sweet flavoured beans are very versatile and can be bought precooked in tins.

SOYA BEANS

Recorded use of soya beans is found from as far back as 1100 BC in China. This ancient food ingredient is very important for vegetarians, as it contains complete protein. Soya beans come in a spectrum of colours – ranging between yellow, green, red and black.

Miso: From Japan, miso is made by cooking the beans and then fermenting them for several months. Use as a flavouring for soups, sauces and stews.

Soy flour: The beans are ground into a flour which is high in protein and low in starch. So while it cannot be used as a normal thickener, it can be added to sauces and gravies to add bulk and useful nutrients.

Soy sauce: Traditionally associated with Chinese food, a useful flavouring which can be added to many recipes, particularly pulse or rice dishes.

Soya milk: This milk is especially useful for vegans or for those who are intolerant to cow's milk. Rich in protein and low in fat, it has a lovely creamy taste.

Tempeh: Again another form of fermented soya beans, this time a bean cake from Indonesia.

Tofu: This traditional Japanese bean curd is available in soft, firm and silken forms, and may be eaten on its own or used in soups, sauces and dressings. Tofu absorbs flavours well and benefits from being marinaded before use.

TVP: Textured vegetable protein was actually designed as a meat substitute, containing complete proteins but without the saturated fat. Useful for recent vegetarians while building up their repertoire of dishes, or when cooking for meat eaters.

Yuba: These are dried bean curd strips. They have to be soaked before use but make an interesting addition to vegetable stews.

SPLIT PEAS

Available in yellow or green, the split and skinned variety of dried peas cook quickly. They make an excellent purée for serving with vegetables, or use to make the British dish of pease pudding. Split pea flour is also now available.

Nuts

ALMONDS
A good source of protein, several important minerals including zinc and iron, and vitamin E. Eat straight from the shell or with their dark skins on for the most nutrients. Ground almonds can be added to any number of sweet and savoury dishes.

BRAZILS
Grown on tall forest trees in South America in large pods that contain between twelve and twenty-four nuts. Eat as a fast-food snack or in salads.

CASHEWS
Native to America, on the trees they grow attached to a fleshy, apple-like fruit. A good vegetarian source of the essential amino acid, lysine, which is more commonly found in animal produce. High in saturated fat, cashews are best kept as an occasional treat.

CHESTNUTS
Containing less natural oil and more starch than other nuts they are more suitable for cooking, stuffings and pâtés. Chestnuts are delicious added to vegetable dishes such as Brussels sprouts or parsnips.

COCONUTS
Buy coconuts that you can hear the liquid inside when you shake them. Use this milk in shakes, or in curry sauces, and the flesh in all sorts of sweet dishes.

HAZELNUTS
Also known as the cob nut, which grows wild in Britain. Lowest in fat of all the nuts and rich in vitamin E, hazelnuts are well worth including in the diet.

MACADAMIA NUTS

Native to Australia, they are sometimes called Queensland nuts.
Serve as a nibble or in a salad so that the delicate flavour can be
appreciated.

PEANUTS

Not really nuts at all, belonging to the same legume family as the
soya bean. They are especially rich in protein, iron, vitamin E, B
vitamins and folic acid. Eat in peanut butter or as a snack fresh
from their shells.

PECANS

Pecan nuts are used a lot in American cooking, especially in the
pudding pecan pie. Their mealy texture makes them useful for
savoury dishes as well.

PINE NUTS

Containing the most protein of all the nuts, pine nuts are the
seed of the stone pine. They have a fresh, creamy appearance
and delicate flavour. Eat them solo, or in omelettes, rice pilaffs
and salads.

PISTACHIO NUTS

A very distinctive flavour and an unusual green colour, they
are ideal to sprinkle onto dishes. These nuts are a useful source
of iron.

WALNUTS

Walnuts are high in calcium and have an unusually strong
flavour that is perfect for tossing into the classic Waldorf salad
along with slices of chopped apple and celery.

Fruits

APPLE

'An apple a day keeps the doctor away' – or it would certainly help. Our favourite fruit contains beta-carotene, vitamin C and some minerals. They also contain acids which neutralise the by-products of indigestion, help cope with excess protein and have pectin to keep our cholesterol levels stable. Eat plain as the ultimate healthy nibble, grate onto cereal, chop into salads or cook into savoury dishes.

APRICOT

Beta-carotene is a natural pigment that gives apricots their bright orange colour. They are also a rich source of vitamin C, potassium and calcium, and dried apricots contain useful amounts of iron.

BANANA

Bananas are nature's own form of fast food, easy to carry, easy to eat. Currently our second most popular fruit, they have high levels of potassium, fibre and also contain magnesium, phosphorus, beta-carotene, folic acid and vitamin C.

BLACKCURRANTS

One of our richest sources of vitamin C. The pigments found in the black skins have antibacterial and anti-inflammatory properties, explaining why blackcurrant juice with a little hot water is especially soothing for sore throats.

BLUEBERRIES

Sometimes known as bilberries or huckleberries, they are a useful cure for diarrhoea. Possibly due to their pectin content they have also been linked to low cholesterol levels.

CITRUS FRUITS

Grapefruit: A Roman writer classified this fruit as a medicine because of its health-giving properties, now known to be vitamin C. Grapefruit also contains potassium, calcium, phosphorus and beta-carotene so is a wonderfully healthy way to begin the day.

Lemon: They contain bioflavonoids in their skins and pulp, but most of the fruits are coated with a wax containing a fungicide, so scrub them well with diluted washing-up liquid before use or buy organically grown ones. Lemon juice and zest, with high levels of vitamin C, are wonderful for flavouring both sweet and savoury dishes.

Lime: In 1775, the globe-trotting discoverer Cook included these fruits as part of his crew's rations, preventing the onset of the often fatal scurvy and giving rise to the sailor's nickname of 'limey'. Use in sauces, as a garnish, or in the top of a bottle of Mexican beer.

Oranges: This most obviously named fruit is one of our most common sources of the antioxidant vitamin C which has been shown to play a valuable role in the prevention of cancers and other degenerative diseases. Fresh orange juice also increases iron absorption by up to three times.

Ugli fruit: A hybrid of the tangerine and the grapefruit, looking more similar to grapefruit, but smaller with sweeter flesh and fewer pips.

CHERRIES

Another store-house of vitamin C, buy in summer and stock up for the year as they freeze well. Lovely cooked in crumbles and stews, fresh with yoghurt or eat a handful as they are.

CRANBERRIES

In addition to beta-carotene, vitamin C, iron and potassium, cranberries also contain unique bacteria-fighting substances that can help treat urinary tract infections, including the painful cystitis. Just one small glass of cranberry juice a day can ward off urinary tract and bladder infections in those prone to them.

DATES
Bedouin tribes travelled for days across the desert with little more than a handful of dates to keep them going. Naturally sweet and nutritious, both fresh and dried dates make a great snack. High in fibre they help to remove impurities from the system by countering constipation.

FIGS
The Romans were fond of feasting on figs and also ate them for health. Modern-day research has isolated an anticancer chemical, benzaldehyde, in figs. In addition they contain beta-carotene, vitamin C, potassium, calcium, the enzyme ficin that aids digestion and plenty of natural fibre. They act as a mild laxative.

GRAPES AND CURRANTS, RAISINS AND SULTANAS
Grapes are mostly water with traces of vitamins and minerals, notably potassium, making them excellent internal cleansers. Occasional one-day grape fasts are a useful way to detoxify the system. Currants, raisins and sultanas are all dried grapes. Sweet but healthy they are a perfect nibble and an essential ingredient in many desserts.

GUAVA
The fruit of the guayaba tree have sunny yellow skins. Guavas have a sharp taste so are best stewed with other fruit. A useful source of vitamin C.

KIWI
Known as the Chinese gooseberry until the New Zealanders

hijacked it in the seventies and exported the 'kiwi' to nouvelle cuisine restaurants around the world. Despite its slightly shabby fur coat, the kiwi is full of goodness, containing vitamin C, beta-carotene, potassium, calcium and phosphorus.

MANGO
Containing high levels of beta-carotene with useful amounts of vitamin C and potassium, its greeny-red skin has become a familiar sight in the supermarket over recent years.

MELON
Several varieties are commonly available: the honeydew melon has a tough yellow casing and is shaped like a rugby ball; the galia melon is smaller and surrounded by a buff-coloured webbing; the cantaloupe melons, including the charentais, are small and orange-fleshed; the ogden has yellow skin and pale green flesh. Their nutritional values vary according to type, but as with all fruit are valuable sources of vitamins and minerals.

PAPAYA
The salmon-pink flesh of the papaya or paw-paw has a tender texture and melt-in-the-mouth consistency, similar to the avocado. Contains beta-carotene, vitamin C, potassium, some calcium and the enzyme papain, which helps digest protein.

PASSION FRUIT
Despite its sexy name, passion fruit is known more for spirituality than sensuality as it was named by Catholic priests after the crucifixion or 'passion' of Christ. Inside the fruit is a spoonful of yellow pips in a scented, cerise substance which contains B vitamins, beta-carotene, vitamin C, potassium and phosphorus.

PEACH
Peaches were first cultivated over four thousand years ago but

have only been available in Britain during this century. An excellent source of the antioxidant beta-carotene, with useful amounts of potassium and phosphorus.

PEAR

This British staple contains significant amounts of beta-carotene, vitamin C and potassium. Pear is delicious raw or cooked and works particularly well with nut and pulse dishes.

PINEAPPLE

This tropical delicacy is really a cluster of tiny fruits that bond together as they grow. Containing many nutrients, notably beta-carotene, folic acid, vitamin C, potassium, calcium and magnesium, fresh pineapple also contains the enzyme bromalin which counteracts bacterium, helps to keep the gut free from infection and aids the digestion of protein.

PLUMS AND PRUNES

Rich in beta-carotene, potassium and phosphorus with some vitamin C. Many different varieties are available from late spring to early autumn. My own favourite is the sweet green-gage. Prunes (dried plums) are infamous for their laxative effect caused by a peculiar chemical composition, so are a good natural cure for constipation.

POMEGRANATE

A large, thick-skinned berry, a pomegranate has an unusual structure of seeds surrounded by shiny, bright red pulp divided into pockets of skin. These sweet, juicy nuggets make an attractive topping.

RHUBARB

Technically an edible stem and not a fruit, rhubarb is a time-honoured internal cleanser and natural tonic, with reasonable amounts of beta-carotene, folic acid and vitamin C. The stewed fruit on its own can be quite bitter, so you may want to mix it with other fruits or bake in a crumble.

SOFT FRUITS

Blackberries: Mentioned by the Ancient Greek 'father of medicine' Hippocrates as both a food and a medicine, blackberries are a good source of vitamin C and taste marvellous with apple or as a dark coulis.

Raspberries: Rich in vitamin C, raspberries also contain useful amounts of potassium and calcium. Raspberries should be on every convalescent's menu, being a fruit that is particularly easy to digest.

Strawberries: Another fund of vitamin C, they also contain beta-carotene, potassium, calcium, iodine and pectin. Strawberries are the perfect and traditional accompaniment to champagne.

Vegetables

ALFALFA

These are bought as seeds, and sprouted before eating, releasing the valuable nutrients. Alfalfa contains complete protein, calcium, B vitamins (including B12) and several enzymes to improve digestion. Use therapeutically as a tonic, a mild diuretic and intestinal cleanser.

ARTICHOKE, GLOBE

A particular favourite of Henry VIII, who claimed they were aphrodisiacs. The globe artichoke is a member of the daisy family and its edible heart contains protein, calcium, iron and potassium. Artichokes also contain insulin which regulates blood sugar.

ASPARAGUS
Asparagus is a member of the lily family and is unusual because it has both male and female plants. As well as a delicious taste, asparagus is an excellent source of beta-carotene, vitamin C and contains some vitamin E and iron.

AUBERGINE
This shiny, purple vegetable is the essential ingredient in ratatouille. Aubergines need salting before cooking to draw out any bitterness or excess moisture.

AVOCADO
Technically a fruit, avocados are unique because half their weight is made up of natural oil, which fortunately is monounsaturated and therefore healthy. A useful source of potassium, vitamin B3 (niacin), vitamin E, beta-carotene and iron. Add to salads for a contrasting taste and texture, or simply scoop it straight out of the skin with a spoon.

BEANS, DRIED — SEE PULSES.

BEETROOT
The first beetroot recipes date back to fifteenth-century English cooking. A good source of beta-carotene, vitamin C, iron, calcium, potassium and magnesium. Grate into salads or bake whole.

BROAD BEAN
Usually it is the shelled beans that are eaten, but the young pods can be eaten if tender enough. Fresh broad beans are only available in summer. Eat them raw or boiled.

BROCCOLI
This vegetable is in fact large stems covered in edible flowers. High in beta-carotene and vitamin C with useful

amounts of calcium. Eat raw with a dip or lightly steamed with some nutmeg.

BRUSSELS SPROUTS
Don't overcook your sprouts as not only do you lose valuable nutrients but you will also spoil that wonderful, crisp taste. Brussels sprouts are traditionally served as a vegetable at Christmas lunch, but are delicious at any time. Their taste combines particularly well with nuts.

CABBAGE
A favourite with naturopaths, cabbage is often served as a tonic and cabbage juice helps stomach ulcers. There are many different varieties of cabbage; the darker the leaves the more nutritious. Steam or stir-fry to keep it crisp.

CARROTS
We have a particular passion for carrots and Britain is the largest worldwide consumer per person. An important group of vitamins called the carotenoids were so called because they were first found in carrots. One of these, beta-carotene, is an antioxidant which can help protect the body from cancer and other degenerative diseases. Traditionally these vegetables are supposed to help you see in the dark.

CAULIFLOWER
Composed of underdeveloped but edible flower buds, this vegetable is a good source of vitamin C, but has few other nutrients. Eat raw with a dip, steamed as a contrast to a deeply coloured dish or as cauliflower cheese.

CELERIAC
This bulbous white root vegetable is a hybrid of celery, hence its name. Celeriac is a useful source of vitamin C and is delicious

raw. Crisp, crunchy and stringless, celeriac is a perfect ingredient for salads and home-made coleslaw.

CELERY

This shoot vegetable is closely related to parsley and both are used by herbalists as a diuretic and natural laxative. Celery juice is used to balance the nervous system and is even reputed to restore a flagging sex drive.

CHICORY

Sometimes called endive, this shoot vegetable is slightly bitter when raw. It can be used in a salad or serve braised.

COURGETTES

Courgettes contain beta-carotene, vitamin C, vitamin B (niacin) and potassium. Courgettes should be crisp and tender and can be eaten raw or lightly fry them in olive oil with a hint of garlic.

CUCUMBERS

The cucumber originated in India where it was heralded as a symbol of fertility. Contains some vitamin C, potassium and other trace elements such as silicon and sulphur. The very high water content, means it is a useful diuretic.

FENNEL

In mediaeval times bunches of fennel were hung outside houses to ward off witches. Fennel is a natural digestive reputed to soothe an irritated stomach and have a mild diuretic action. Lightly steam or eat raw.

GREEN BEANS

There are several varieties of these beans including French and runner beans. Native to Central America, the latter are grown for their whole pod and contents.

JERUSALEM ARTICHOKES
Ideal alternatives to potatoes, these knobbly tubers contain a high percentage of starch. Jerusalem artichokes are one of the tastiest tubers and come from a plant related to the sunflower.

LAMB'S LETTUCE
Also known as corn salad, the leaves have a delicate, slightly bitter flavour and are a good contrast taste in salads. They are also fun as a garnish and make a delicious soup.

LEEKS
When the Welsh went into battle against the Saxons in 640 AD, they wore leeks to distinguish themselves from the English. Wales won and the leek was adopted as a national emblem and is still worn on St David's Day. These relatives of the onion are especially rich in potassium and can help eliminate uric acid from the system, so are particularly good for arthritis sufferers.

LETTUCE
Wild lettuce has a milky white juice containing narcotic substances, explaining why Beatrix Potter's Peter Rabbit fell asleep in Mr McGregor's garden after feasting on his tender lettuces. Salads made with lettuce leaves have been popular in Britain since the Middle Ages. Pick darker varieties of lettuce for more nutrients.

MANGE-TOUT
A variety of pea eaten complete with pod when young and tender. Steam lightly or add to stir-frys to retain the crisp texture and delicate flavour.

MUSHROOMS
Cultivated mushrooms contain traces of iron, B vitamins and potassium. Don't pick wild mushrooms unless you know

exactly what to look for as some varieties are highly poisonous. All fungi should be avoided by those with candidiasis (thrush) as the spores can aggravate this fungal condition.

OKRA

Sometimes more elegantly known as Lady's Fingers. Okra is lovely added to soups, stews and curries, especially when cooked with spices to mask the slimy texture of this vegetable.

OLIVES

The olive branch is a traditional symbol of peace and hope, carried by the dove to Noah's Ark. Actually a fruit, the olive is used extensively in Mediterranean food. The only difference between green and black olives is that the black ones are fully ripened.

ONIONS

Contain naturally antiseptic oils, one of which helps the walls of blood vessels dissolve clots which form inside them. Onions are essential to many savoury recipes, but unfortunately can cause you to cry as you chop them. Try chopping them under water or leave slicing off the root end till last.

PARSNIP

This close relative of the carrot used to be a staple of the British diet before being largely replaced by the potato in the nineteenth century. A useful source of vitamin C, parsnips have a sweet, nutty flavour and are delicious baked in their skins.

PEAS

Although fresh peas available in summer have a particularly good flavour, most of us find it more convenient to buy the frozen variety. Cooked in seconds they are an easy way to add colour and interest to any plate.

PEPPERS

This vegetable was misnamed by Christopher Columbus in his search for peppercorns. Sweet peppers come in the three traffic light colours, red, yellow and green, and contain beta-carotene and plenty of vitamin C.

POTATOES

Brought to the British Isles by the great explorers of the Elizabethan era, potatoes are now one of the staples of our diet. Eat potatoes either baked (a serving of chips has three times the calories and twelve times the fat) or boiled in their skins to obtain all the fibre and vitamin C.

PUMPKIN

A wonderful bright orange colour, this vegetable can be boiled, fried or puréed. Buy before Halloween and use the hollowed-out skin to make pumpkin-head candle holders.

RADISH

Rich in vitamin C and the amyclytic enzyme which is useful in urinary tract disorders and is said to prevent gallstones. If you cut a radish four or six times almost to the base and place in a bowl of ice-cold water it will open up like a flower.

SEA VEGETABLES

Seaweeds are some of the oldest vegetables known to mankind.
Agar-agar: Sold in the form of flakes or threads made by freeze-drying a red Japanese seaweed called tengusa. Agar-agar contains alginates which are powerful gelling agents and so it is a vegetarian alternative to gelatine.
Arame: With a milk flavour, these thin strips can be soaked and added to noodles or mixed with other vegetables.
Dulse: A traditional Irish sea vegetable, this purple-coloured seaweed is rich in iron and has a slightly spicy flavour.

Hiziki: These glistening black strips of seaweed are rich in many minerals, particularly calcium and iron, and have a strong flavour. Serve with stir-fried tofu and sesame seeds or cook the strips in boiling water and use instead of spaghetti.

Kombu: Kombu or kelp is rich in iodine and contains glutamic acid. Cooking beans and pulses with kombu helps to tenderise them by softening their fibres, making them more digestible.

Nori: One of the tastiest of all sea vegetables, sold shredded or in thin square sheets for wrapping around rice balls. Nori is extremely high in iron and beta-carotene – no kitchen should be without it!

Wakame: A close relative of kelp, wakame is another great flavour-enhancer and tenderiser but has a milder flavour. Used in the traditional Japanese miso soup.

SPAGHETTI SQUASH

This yellow vegetable is shaped like a rugby ball. It gets its name from its stringy fibrous inside that can be served as a gluten-free alternative to spaghetti. Rich in beta-carotene, B vitamins and potassium.

SPINACH

Folic acid, especially important during pregnancy as it guards against spina bifida and anencephaly, was first identified in spinach. Although spinach is rich in iron (remember Popeye?) it is the vegetable form which is difficult to absorb. Eat young, tender spinach raw in salads, steam it or bake it in the oven as a gratin.

SPRING ONIONS

One of the gentler relations of the onion family, their milder taste gives a bit of a kick to salads and other dishes as a garnish.

SWEETCORN

Boil fresh sweetcorn with a knob of butter melted over each one – always an ice-breaker as they can be quite tricky to eat!

SWEET POTATOES

These starchy tubers are not related to potatoes although they can be used in the same way. A useful source of beta-carotene, vitamin C, calcium and iron. Their natural sweetness makes them especially popular with babies and children.

TOMATOES

A relatively common culprit of food intolerance which can trigger skin rashes. But tomatoes are good sources of beta-carotene and vitamin C. Great in salads and a staple of many sauces, particularly in Italian cooking.

TURNIP

Turnip leaves contain more calcium than any other vegetable, so are especially important for vegans. Turnip tops are also an excellent source of beta-carotene, vitamin C, B vitamins, magnesium, sulphur, iodine and iron. The more commonly found root, while still being healthy, is nowhere near as full of goodies.

WATERCRESS

The Romans first used watercress leaves as a medicine, not a food. Watercress contain sulphur, calcium, iron, B vitamins, vitamin C and iodine. Add lavishly to salads. A watercress garnish is an easy way of enriching any dish with extra vitamins.

Vegetable Oils

CORN OIL

Also known as maize oil, it is extracted from sweetcorn kernels and is one of the cheapest oils available. High in polyunsaturates, corn oil deteriorates at high temperatures so use in cold dressings.

GRAPESEED OIL

Extracted from grape pips, the areas of production unsurprisingly coincide with the great wine regions. Hard to find in an unrefined version, but if you can it has one of the highest contents of polyunsaturated fatty acids.

GROUNDNUT OIL

Extracted from peanut kernels, it is sometimes called peanut oil. Hard to find in an unrefined form, the refined oil is stripped of valuable nutrients during processing.

HAZELNUT OIL

High in monounsaturates, it has the lowest saturated fat content of any cooking oil. Stable at high temperatures, its nutty taste can be particularly useful in baking and yet is also delicious raw.

OLIVE OIL

The culinary superstar that no kitchen should be without. Monounsaturated, it is excellent for all types of cooking. Wonderfully healthy, it is known to be a factor leading to the low rates of cancer and heart disease in Mediterranean countries. Rich in vitamin E and lecithin, buy the darker coloured oils which are the least refined and most nutritious.

RAPESEED OIL

Rapeseed is the crop from the bright yellow fields dotted around the countryside. Rapeseed cooking oil is sometimes called canola and is a good source of healthy monosaturates.

SAFFLOWER OIL

The safflower is related to the thistle. The oil is extracted from the seeds and is an excellent source of polyunsaturated fatty acids. A light, slightly nutty taste, use cold in dressings.

SESAME OIL

Popular since Roman times, this oil is monounsaturated and so can safely be heated. Toasted it is an essential ingredient to many Chinese dishes, but this form contains a high level of potentially damaging peroxides.

SOYBEAN OIL

As the soya bean contains less than 20 percent oil, some manufacturers use solvent extraction so always buy unrefined soybean oil to avoid the hexane and to obtain an excellent source of vitamin E and lecithin. As with all polyunsaturates it should not be heated to high temperatures.

SUNFLOWER OIL

From the seeds of the plant which takes its name from the huge sun-like flowers. Sunflower oil is rich in polyunsaturates, has a mild, sweet flavour and is excellent for using cold or warm.

WALNUT OIL

A great favourite with French chefs for centuries who even use walnut oil to fry eggs, a few drops can transform an ordinary salad dressing into something special. Walnut oil is high in polyunsaturated fatty acids.

Herbs, Spices and Seeds

ALLSPICE

So-called because it tastes like a mixture of cinnamon, pepper and cloves. An essential ingredient of Christmas pudding. Used in tonics and digestives.

BASIL

Basil is a sacred herb in India that is used to cleanse and purify and is reputedly good for headaches. It is high in beta-carotene, calcium and iron. Basil is used extensively in Italian cooking as it complements tomatoes, pasta and rich cheeses.

BAY
Bought as complete leaves, bay contains oils which are mildly narcotic and have been used to soothe tension and hysteria. Bay is said to stimulate the appetite and its mellow flavour suits grain dishes.

BLACK PEPPER
A type of vine pepper native to Asia but now used extensively in cooking all around the globe. Best freshly ground so that it adds taste as well as heat and a pepper mill is an attractive addition to any table or kitchen.

CAPER
Capers are an unopened flower bud. Used in their pickled form, these have a strong flavour that you will either love or hate. A tasty addition to pizzas and salads.

CARAWAY SEEDS
The Greek physician Discorides prescribed caraway seeds for 'girls of pale face'. Used in German and Jewish cookery, caraway seeds are delicious with cabbage, cauliflower or added to rye bread and baked apples.

CARDAMOM PODS
From Sri Lanka, the pods should be cracked to release the seeds before using. Highly aromatic, a small amount of cardamom powder will go a long way and can be used to flavour both sweet and savoury dishes.

CAROB POWDER
A flavouring which comes from the pulp of the carob bean. This

is particularly useful as a flavouring for puddings and sweets, as it offers a healthier alternative to chocolate.

CAYENNE PEPPER

This type of pepper is hotter than black pepper and should be used with care. Excellent for use in curries and chillies.

CHERVIL

This herb resembles parsley but it has a more subtle flavour. Chervil can be mixed with other mild-flavoured herbs and used in grain dishes. Sprigs of fresh chervil are also good in salads.

CHILLIES

These can be bought fresh, dried or ground into a pepper. Used in spicy, hot dishes for their heat, particularly the vegetarian version of the dish of the same name – chilli.

CHIVES

A relative of the onion, but it is the stalks not the roots which are used. Chives are wonderfully easy to grow and will thrive in a pot in the kitchen or in a window box. They are excellent chopped into salads or mixed with other herbs for savoury dishes.

CINNAMON

Cinnamon comes from the inner bark of a species of laurel tree, the sticks are actually scrapings which curl up when dried in the sun. Used by herbalists as a tonic, small doses can improve the blood circulation. Delicious added to many fruit dishes, rice puddings and sweet breads.

CLOVES

The tiny dried buds come from an evergreen tree in Indonesia. Cloves should be used sparingly but are excellent when used to flavour fruit and sauces. Essential when making bread and butter pudding.

CORIANDER

As a herb both the stalks and leaves are used in cooking and have a slightly bitter, pungent flavour. Reputedly an aphrodisiac, coriander can be added to many savoury dishes and gives a subtle flavour to cooked fruits, muffins and mousses.

CUMIN

Cumin seeds are popular in Middle Eastern cookery. They have a pungent, bitter flavour and a distinctive aroma. Useful for stimulating the appetite and soothing the digestion, cumin works best with savoury dishes.

DILL AND DILL SEEDS

Herbalists use dill to treat insomnia. The delicate, feathery leaves of this herb are a traditional accompaniment to egg dishes. Also delicious chopped into potato salads or added to coleslaws. The crushed seeds have been used for centuries to relieve flatulence and infant colic. In addition to soothing the stomach, dill seeds are excellent for flavouring salad dressings.

FENNEL SEEDS

Dried fennel seeds have an unusual aniseed taste and are often used in Italian cooking. Use in both sweet and savoury dishes especially in mild curries, or with fruits such as apple. Reputed to make pulses easier to digest.

GARLIC

This most powerful member of the onion family has many unusual properties. The garlic bulb grabs sulphurs from the soil as it grows, these sulphur compounds act as internal antibacterial and antifungal agents, preventing stomach upsets. It helps regulate blood fats such as cholesterol and strengthens your immune system so helping to ward off all those bugs and colds. Garlic is a useful flavouring which can be used in many savoury dishes.

GINGER
This spicy underground stem, or rhizome, may be bought fresh or dried but the freshly grated root has a better flavour. Ginger can be added to many sweet and savoury dishes, working well with root vegetables, cabbage, grains, melons and other fruits. Essential to Chinese herbal medicine, it thins the blood and lowers cholesterol levels, acts as a painkiller, and can cure nausea.

HORSERADISH
This is the richest plant source of sulphur. Horseradish is used in herbal medicine to treat the liver and tone the system and it also has antibiotic qualities and can clear catarrh.

JUNIPER
Juniper berries take three years to ripen and are used to make gin, giving it its unique flavour. Add to casseroles and vegetable dishes.

LEMON GRASS
The term lemon grass covers several varieties of grass which have similar lemony flavours due to the presence of citrus oils. Used extensively in Thai cookery.

LIQUORICE
A flavouring with a long history, liquorice is a root with a sweet-sour taste which we associate predominantly with confectionery. However, it is a taste worth experimenting with in other dishes.

MARJORAM

Marjoram is very similar to oregano, but is a slightly gentler flavour. It combines particularly well with cheese and grain dishes. This herb contains high levels of thymol, a powerful antioxidant.

MINT

Both mint and spearmint were brought to Britain by the Romans and have been used extensively in British cooking ever since. The herb acts as both a breath-freshener and digestive, and the seventeenth-century herbalist Culpeper maintained mint was 'comfortable for the head and memory'.

MUSTARD

Mustard as we know it is a mixture of white, black and brown mustard seeds ground up with some flour and turmeric and then blended with cold water. Various varieties of mustard are made by using whole seeds or by adding herbs or green peppercorns.

NUTMEG

Nutmegs are best bought whole and grated as required to preserve their flavour. Excellent with sauces, custards, egg dishes and stewed fruits. Use sparingly, especially when cooking for children as they contain myristicin, a toxic substance.

OREGANO

The name comes from the Greek words meaning 'joy of the mountains'. Oregano contains the antioxidant thymol. Widely used in Italian cooking, it is a herb that blends well with tomatoes so is particularly useful for pasta sauces and pizza toppings.

PAPRIKA

The flavour of this red pepper is milder than other types of pepper and is good for adding colour and flavour to pulse and grain dishes.

PARSLEY

Parsley can be a difficult herb to grow, although it is said to flourish in households where the woman is in charge. Fresh parsley is rich in many vitamins and minerals and is a nutritious garnish or topping to almost every savoury dish. Herbalists prize parsley for its diuretic action and also use it as a liver tonic.

POPPY SEEDS

Poppies became notorious after the discovery of opium. Poppy seeds used for cooking do not contain narcotics. An important part of Jewish cookery, poppy seeds can be added to breads, biscuits, rice and grain dishes.

PUMPKIN SEEDS

Long linked in folklore to male virility, these dark green seeds contain useful amounts of iron, zinc and calcium, as well as some protein and B vitamins.

ROSEMARY

This highly scented herb is dedicated to friendship and sprigs were woven into Elizabethan wedding garlands. Herbalists use rosemary to treat disorders of the head, induce menstruation, raise blood pressure and boost the circulation.

SAFFRON

The vivid yellow strands come from the saffron crocus. An expensive spice as around 50,000 hand-picked stamens are needed to produce each pound of saffron. Saffron gives savoury dishes a mildly aromatic flavour but is used mainly to dye foods such as bread and rice a vivid shade of yellow.

SAGE

Reputed to increase powers of concentration. This aromatic herb has a pungent flavour which complements heavier foods particularly well and acts as a digestive. Excellent with all types of cheese, egg and grain dishes.

SESAME SEEDS

An outstanding source of calcium and a rich source of protein. These tiny seeds also contains plenty of vitamin E, lecithin, iron and zinc. Versatile, a handful can be added to almost any recipe. Use to make milk-free shakes or grind them into a thick sesame butter called tahini.

SUNFLOWER SEEDS

These naturally sweet seeds contain generous amounts of protein, vitamins B and E, iron, magnesium, zinc, fibre and essential fatty acids. Almost half the sunflower seed is taken up with polyunsaturates which keeps our cholesterol levels in check.

TAMARIND

The dried fruit of the tamarind tree is sold as broken pods. Known as 'Indian dates' because of its fibrous, sticky texture, tamarind is often added to curries to give sharpness.

TARRAGON

Used extensively in French cookery, tarragon leaves have a distinctive, spicy flavour. It gives an excellent flavour to many vegetable dishes and is useful for flavouring soups and sauces.

THYME

Another herb brought to Britain by the Romans and tradition-ally it symbolises courage. Culpeper referred to it fighting on a different front – that of infections. In cooking, the strong flavour of thyme complements richer foods. In contrast, a few leaves will subtly flavour a salad dressing.

TURMERIC

A rhizome or underground stem from the ginger family, turmeric is the basic ingredient of curry powder. It is used in herbal medicine as a stimulant and can also be used in cooking as a yellow dye.

VANILLA

The long dark pods from this climbing orchid plant are dried and used mainly to scent and flavour sweet dishes such as custards, mousses and yoghurts. Although the dried pods are expensive, they can be rinsed and reused many times and taste a good deal better than synthetic vanilla essence.

Dairy and Dairy Products

CHEESE

Despite the huge number of cheeses available, there are in fact fewer varieties than in previous times when cheese was produced individually by each farmhouse and was local in the truest sense of the word. Although cow's milk accounts for the majority of cheeses, goat's and sheep's milk cheeses are produced in Europe and the Middle East. There are even cheeses produced from such diverse animals as the yak, the reindeer, the buffalo and the donkey.

Fresh or unripened cheeses: These cheeses have a milder taste than most and may sometimes even be quite bland. However, this makes them great to eat with summer salads and fresh crusty bread, or to use as a base of a dip or in cooking. The low-fat soft cheeses such as quark or low-fat cottage cheese are good substitutes for higher fat dairy products. Curd cheese is the traditional cheese to use in cheese cakes while cream cheese tastes wonderful in sandwiches and salads. The Italian soft cheeses such as ricotta and mozzarella are great with pasta, and mozzarella is the ultimate pizza topping. Alternatively buy fresh cheese with herbs in the French pinwheel roule.

Soft cheeses: Briefly ripened, soft cheeses are, as their name suggests, soft and easy to spread. They make an excellent contrast to hard cheeses on a cheese board and taste good chopped into salads, or melted over foods. Brie or camembert are delicious deep-fried and served with cranberry sauce. Feta cheese is needed to make the classic Greek salad. Chèvre or goat's milk cheeses come in a whole range of flavours depending on their maturity – try grilling on top of tomatoes and serving on a crisp bed of lettuce.

Semi-hard and hard cheeses: These are the cheeses that are not spreadable and need cutting instead. This section includes probably our best known cheese – Cheddar. The flavours of Cheddar are wide-ranging and this together with its adaptability make it so popular. Edam with its distinctive red skin is useful for being slightly lower in fat than many other cheeses. Or try the stronger tasting cheeses, such as Gruyère, Manchego or Parmesan, to cut down on fat as you need far less to achieve a good flavour. Use Cheshire or Lancashire to crumble into a salad, or Double Gloucester or Red Leicester for their appetising colour. The classic holey cheese is Emmenthal and it makes a wonderful cheese fondue. An unusual tasting cheese is Caerphilly, which comes from Wales and has a mild, slightly sour taste which contrasts well with other sweeter cheeses.

Blue cheeses: Cheeses such as Stilton, Roquefort, Danish Blue and Gorgonzola are ripened with a mould culture added into the cheese to create the blue streaks. They have a very strong taste which many people love on their own, but they are particularly useful in dips and sauces. They also go well with pears on a cheese board.

CREAM

This is the fatty part of milk which rises to the surface when the milk is left standing. The concentration varies from single cream 18 percent fat, through soured cream, whipping cream, double cream, to clotted cream which is a huge 55 percent fat. Thick creams contain lots of saturated fat, so should be avoided except for the occasional treat.

Crème frâiche: A sharp tasting cream, which is excellent for cooking as it doesn't separate or curdle when heated.

Butter (and margarine): The well-known spreading butter is made from cream, but it is high in saturated fat and if you eat a lot it might be worth replacing with vegetable oils in cooking or a low-fat spreading margarine. In fact, most margarines are technically not dairy products at all as they are made from vegetable oils (so are suitable for vegans).

Smetana: This is a low-fat soured cream and is especially useful to replace soured cream in both sweet and savoury recipes, thus cutting down on saturated fat.

Soured cream: This is cream which has had a lactic acid culture added to give it a slightly acid flavour.

EGGS

Eggs have often been seen as a symbol of fertility. They also represented rebirth and therefore the resurrection to the early Christians, hence the custom of giving chocolate eggs at Easter. All birds produce eggs, but it is the domestic hen's eggs which are most usually eaten. Although there is no nutritional difference it is better to buy free-range eggs because of the atrocities suffered by battery hens. The egg is packed full of proteins but also contains a good deal of cholesterol. They are well worth including in the diet, but not every day. Eggs can be eaten boiled, poached, fried, scrambled and used to make omelettes. They are also used as an ingredient in many recipes because of the interesting ways in which they behave. When whipped, egg whites break down and expand by trapping air, which in turn expands if subjected to heat. This makes egg white a particularly useful leavening agent. Egg yolk, on the other hand, acts as a binding and thickening agent. Other eggs which are regularly eaten include duck's eggs, which must be well cooked as they can absorb bacteria, and quail's eggs which are generally eaten cold after hardboiling.

MILK

Milk is the basis of all dairy products. Packed full of nutrients including complete protein, calcium, riboflavin and vitamins A, D and B12, milk is available with the natural amount of milk remaining (full fat), semi-skimmed or skimmed. As much of the fat is saturated, it is better to use one of the reduced fat versions (with the exception of small children, below three years' old, who should always be given full-fat milk). Milk can also be bought in powdered form, which is simply dehydrated milk. This is a good store-cupboard item for emergencies or for adding to drinks. When we say milk, we normally mean cow's milk. However, cow's milk is a relatively common allergen. Sometimes those who are sensitive to it do not react to goat's or sheep's milk so these can be worth trying. Often a better alternative is to use soya milk and other products, such as margarine and cheese.

Homogenised milk: This is whole milk which has been processed so that the cream does not separate out. It is therefore particularly useful for some recipes where the milk might separate.

Pasteurised milk: Almost all of the milk we buy, including that delivered to the doorstep, is pasteurised. This means that it is heated to 71°C (160°F) for fifteen seconds to destroy bacteria. Raw milk is available from good health shops and is not heat-treated.

Sterilised milk: Sold as long-life milk, this has been heated to far higher temperatures than pasteurised milk and consequently keeps for longer. However, sterilisation changes the taste of the milk.

Buttermilk: In its true form, this is the sour milk left over from butter making. However, nowadays it is more commonly made from skimmed milk. Use as a drink, or in baking and confectionery making.

Condensed milk: This is essentially evaporated milk with lots of sugar added before canning. Condensed milk contains large amounts of fat and sugar, with relatively few useful nutrients.

Evaporated milk: Bought in cans, this is milk which has had about half its water content removed by evaporation. A useful topping or cooking ingredient for many puddings.

Yoghurt: This is a product made from curdled milk and is made with the help of a beneficial bacteria. Look for live yoghurt which is very helpful for the digestive system. Many of the yoghurts you can buy in pots contain lots of additives and sugar. I find it tastier and cheaper to buy big pots of plain, natural yoghurt and add fruit, fruit purées or a dash of honey or maple syrup. Plain yoghurt is an excellent topping for many sweet and savoury dishes.

—— 4 ——
Recipes

VEGETARIAN BASICS

Home-made yoghurt: Yoghurt is a versatile vegetarian ingredient with a multitude of sweet and savoury uses. Nutritionally, it is an excellent source of calcium, yet because it is fermented it is more easily digested than cheese or cream. Home-made yoghurt is easy and inexpensive and can be made from any milk, including cow's, goat's, sheep's – skimmed, semi-skimmed or whole according to your fat content preference. Vegans can also make their own yoghurt from soya or nut milk.

To start your first batch of yoghurt you will need a commercially made yoghurt or a culture powder (good for vegans or those with a milk allergy). For successive batches, reserve 2tbsps of the yoghurt you produce for the next batch.

600ml (1 pint) semi-skimmed milk

30ml (2tbsps) plain yoghurt (or 1 sachet of culture powder)

Place the milk in a saucepan and heat to a temperature of 43–44°C (110-115°F). Alternatively, simmer the milk and cool to this temperature. Stir in the yoghurt starter or sachet of culture powder. Pour into a prewarmed wide-neck thermos flask. Leave overnight to set. Transfer to smaller pots or a covered bowl and cool in the fridge. The yoghurt will thicken as it cools. For a slightly thicker consistency, stir in 1tbsp skimmed milk powder together with the yoghurt starter.

Low-fat pastry: Pastry is a valuable vegetarian ingredient as it can be used to encase a wide range of foods. However, it is often high in fat and low in fibre and minerals. This recipe uses wholewheat flour to give more fibre and iron. It is also significantly lower in saturated fat than conventional recipes.

> *175g (6oz) wholewheat flour (organic and conservation*
> *grades have a lower pesticide content)*
> *15ml (1tbsp) buckwheat or soya flour (optional)*
> *pinch of salt*
> *7ml (1¹/₂tsps) baking powder*
> *15ml (1tbsp) olive oil*
> *skimmed or soya milk to mix*

Sift the flours, salt and baking powder into a large bowl. Add the olive oil and sufficient milk to mix to a dough. Cover with a clean cloth and place in the top of the fridge to rest for 10 minutes before rolling out. This is an important part of any pastry-making process as it allows the gluten in the flour to lose its elasticity. When rolling out, try to get the pastry extra thin as wholewheat varieties are denser and more filling than usual.

Strudel pastry: It is worth getting the hang of making strudel pastry as it is delicious served with both sweet and savoury fillings. The trick with this delicate pastry is to knead the dough thoroughly so that it can be stretched out thinly without tearing.

> *150g (5oz) wholewheat flour (organic and conservation*
> *grades have a lower pesticide content)*
> *pinch of salt*
> *15ml (3tsps) olive oil*
> *100ml (4fl oz) water*

Sift the flour and salt into a bowl. Stir in 10ml (2tsps) of the oil with all the water and mix to form a soft dough. Place on a floured surface ready for kneading. Pick up the dough and slap it down in between kneading the mixture with your knuckles and palms. Repeat at least ten times, or until the dough becomes smooth and elastic. Brush the dough ball with the remaining 5ml (1tsp) olive oil, cover with a bowl and leave to 'rest' for 15 minutes. Then, place on a well-floured cloth and flatten with the hands. Gently stretch the dough from the centre until it forms a thin sheet over the cloth. Leave to dry slightly before spreading with your filling and rolling up.

Cooking pulses: Pulses are the mainstay of the vegetarian and vegan store cupboard. Dried pulses are the cheapest and tastiest (and last for ages in the cupboard). To save cooking time, reconstitute more than you need and freeze the extra. Soaking before boiling speeds up the cooking time, but rinse under the tap first and pick over to remove any small stones or grit. Pulses have a reputation for causing wind and this can be avoided by changing the soaking water and boiling in clean, fresh water. Adding a small piece of kombu seaweed also helps to reduce the risk of flatulence. All pulses need boiling for *at least* 20 minutes to neutralise the natural toxins present in all dried pulses.

Table 4 Cooking Pulses

	SOAKING	COOKING
Aduki beans	no need	35–40 minutes
Black-eyed beans	no need	40–50 minutes
Borlotti beans	overnight	60–70 minutes
Butter beans	overnight	1–1½ hours
Chick peas	overnight	2–3 hours
Dried peas	overnight	1½–2 hours
Flageolet beans	overnight	1 hour
Haricot beans	overnight	50–60 minutes
Lentils	no need	30–40 minutes
Red kidney beans	overnight	1½–2 hours
Mung beans	no need	40–50 minutes
Pinto beans	overnight	1½–2 hours
Soya beans	overnight	3½–4 hours

Cooking wholegrains: All rice, millet, buckwheat, barley and quinoa can be prepared as follows. It is best to use the wholegrains with their fibrous and nutritious outer husks, but this also means you should try to use organically grown varieties to avoid pesticides. The idea is to absorb all the cooking liquid so the grain's nutrients are retained. Adding the cooking water from lightly boiled vegetables gives extra flavour and the goodness from water-soluble vitamins B and C that would otherwise be thrown down the sink. Varying the basics by adding sunflower seeds, onions, or dried fruit or herbs turns a simple side dish into an adventurous main course. *Serves 2*

225g (8oz) wholegrain, eg rice, barley, rye, etc
15ml (1tbsp) olive oil
2–3 times the grain's volume of water or vegetable cooking water
1tbsp sunflower seeds (optional)
1 onion, peeled and finely chopped (optional)

All grains must be washed by rinsing them under running tap water in a sieve. In a large saucepan lightly fry the grains in the oil before adding the water. Add the sunflower seeds and finely chopped onion. Cover and bring to the boil, reduce the heat and simmer for 15–30 minutes (depending on the grain) until soft.

Low-fat white sauce: White sauce is an integral part of many savoury dishes and can be adapted for many different recipes. For example, a spoonful of wholegrain mustard gives plain white sauce an extra bite, while a dash of tabasco or Worcestershire sauce adds a subtle piquancy. This recipe is especially useful as it cuts down on the fat without sacrificing flavour.

300ml (¹/2pint) skimmed milk (or soya milk)
1 bay leaf
1 small onion studded with cloves, to taste
15ml (1tbsp) olive oil
25g (1oz) wholewheat flour
pinch of salt and black pepper

Heat the milk in a saucepan together with the bay leaf and onion. Bring to the boil, remove from the heat and allow to stand for 10–15 minutes. Remove the bay leaf and onion and pour the flavoured milk into a jug. In the saucepan, heat the olive oil over a low heat and stir in the flour, mixing continuously. Cook for a few minutes before adding the milk a little at a time. Stir well to ensure a smooth consistency (use a wire whisk to remove any lumps). Bring to the edge of boiling before turning down the heat and simmering gently for 5 minutes. Season with black pepper to taste.

Variations on a theme:

✳ Add 100g (4oz) mixed Gruyère and Cheddar cheeses.

✳ Add 1tbsp each of freshly chopped dill and parsley.

✳ Add 1tbsp capers and 1tsp dried tarragon.

✳ Add 1tsp finely chopped garlic and a sprinkling of grated nutmeg.

Tomato sauce: This rich, tasty sauce can be served alone on pasta or rice, or may be used as a base for casseroling chopped courgettes, mushrooms or Jerusalem artichokes.

120ml (4fl oz) olive oil
300g (10oz) onion, finely chopped
100g (4oz) carrot, chopped
4 cloves garlic, crushed
1kg (2¼lb) tomatoes, chopped or 1 litre (1¾pints) passata (sieved tomatoes)
1tbsp fresh basil, chopped
1tbsp fresh oregano, chopped

Heat the oil in a large saucepan or deep-sided frying pan. Add the onions, carrot and garlic. Stir frequently until the vegetables have softened. Add the chopped tomatoes or passata, cover the pan and simmer over a low heat for 20 minutes. Stir in the chopped herbs, partially cover and simmer for a further 10 minutes.

Vegetable stock: The problem with many commercial stock cubes is that they are high in both salt and additives such as monosodium glutamate. It is easy enough to make your own vegetable stock by reserving the cooking water from vegetables, boosting its flavour with a few chopped herbs and a dash of tamari or shoyu sauce. Alternatively, try this recipe for vegetable stock and keep in small pots in the freezer.

15ml (1tbsp) olive oil
2 large carrots, chopped
1 large onion, chopped
1 bay leaf
1 sprig rosemary or thyme
1 clove garlic, crushed
15ml (1tbsp) miso paste
1.5 litres (1½ pints) water
black pepper to season

Use a large saucepan to fry the vegetables and seasonings lightly in the olive oil. Add the water, cover and bring to the boil. Turn down the heat and simmer for about an hour. Strain the cooking liquor through a sieve and season with pepper to taste.

Soups

Green lentil soup: This thick, creamy soup is delicious served with chunks of crusty bread or rye crackers. It freezes well and is popular with children and adults alike. *Serves 4*

200g (7oz) green lentils, rinsed
1 medium onion, finely chopped
150g (5oz) swede, peeled and chopped
900ml (1½ pints) vegetable stock (see above)
small carton plain bio-yoghurt

Cook the lentils in the vegetable stock. Boil rapidly for 10 minutes, then add the chopped onion and swede. Simmer the lentils and vegetables for 30 minutes, skimming any scum from the lentils with a slotted spoon. Pour into a blender and liquidise, or purée using a hand blender. Serve hot with a swirl of plain yoghurt in each bowl.

Chilled gazpacho: *Serves 4*
    600ml (1 pint) tomato juice
    2 slices wholemeal bread
    2 garlic cloves, crushed
    45ml (3tbsps) olive oil or sunflower oil
    1/2 cucumber
    1 red or green pepper, deseeded
    4 tomatoes, skinned and deseeded
    1 medium onion
    black pepper to season

Pour half the tomato juice into a food processor or blender, pour the remaining half over the bread and leave it to soak. To the tomato juice, add the garlic, cider vinegar and half of each vegetable, roughly chopped. Chop the remaining half very finely ready to add to the soup before serving (or if a completely smooth texture is preferred, add all the vegetables now). Process until smooth, add the soaked bread and process again. Add more tomato juice or water, if necessary, to give the right consistency. Chill before serving, adding the reserved chopped vegetables.

Buckwheat noodle soup: A satisfying soup made with nourishing noodles and kombu seaweed. *Serves 2-3*
    2³⁄₄ litres (5 pints) water plus 350ml (12fl oz) water
    225g (8oz) buckwheat noodles
    8 spring onions, trimmed and finely chopped
    1tbsp olive oil
    750ml (1¹⁄₄ pints) water
    3-inch piece kombu seaweed
    3tbsps tamari sauce

Bring the 2³⁄₄ litres (5 pints) of water to the boil in a large saucepan. Add the buckwheat noodles and bring the water back to the boil, then add 120ml (4fl oz) of the remaining cold water. Repeat the process of bringing the water back to the boil and adding the cold water three times. Take the saucepan off the heat, cover and leave for 10 minutes. Drain and rinse the noodles in cold water and set aside.

Heat the oil in a saucepan and sauté the spring onions for a few minutes. Add the 750ml (1¼ pints) water and the kombu seaweed, and bring to the boil. Cover and simmer for 15 minutes. Remove the kombu seaweed and set on one side. Meanwhile reheat the noodles by pouring boiling water over them. Drain and put the noodles into warmed bowls with the kombu seaweed, and pour the soup over.

Cream of celery soup: This soup has a wonderful smooth texture, but to save time it can also be served leaving out the puréeing stage. *Serves 4–6*

  1 tbsp sesame oil
  2 onions, peeled and finely chopped
  10 stalks celery, chopped
  40g (1½ oz) oat flakes
  1¼ litres (2¼ pints) water
  1 tsp freshly chopped thyme or dill

Heat the sesame oil in a saucepan and sauté for another few minutes. Stir in the oat flakes and gently cook for about 5 minutes until they are well-coated with the sesame oil and moistened. Slowly stir in the water, cover and simmer over a low heat for 30–40 minutes. Purée the soup in a food processor until smooth. Serve sprinkled with the fresh herbs.

STARTERS

Stuffed mushrooms: This dish can be served hot as a starter, or cold as part of an informal buffet. *Serves 4*

225g (8oz) medium mushrooms, wiped
1 small onion
2 garlic cloves
1tbsp walnut, hazelnut or almond oil
75g (3oz) freshly chopped hazelnuts and almonds
50g (2oz) fresh breadcrumbs
50g (2oz) half-fat Cheddar cheese

Preheat the oven to 190°C (375°F, gas mark 5). Remove the mushroom stalks and chop them finely with the onion. Crush the garlic over the mixture and mix well. Heat the nut oil in a saucepan and fry the chopped mixture for a few minutes or until the onion becomes transparent. Remove from the heat and stir in the chopped nuts, breadcrumbs and cheese. Use the mixture to stuff (but not over-fill) the mushroom cups. Bake in the oven for 20 minutes. Serve on a bed of shredded lettuce.

Mushroom pâté: A wonderfully easy starter which also makes a great snack on rice cakes. If possible use the larger varieties of mushrooms, which I find generally have more flavour. *Serves 4–6*

225g (8oz) mushrooms, roughly chopped
1 clove garlic, crushed
1tbsp olive oil
2tbsps white wine
50g (2oz) almonds or hazelnuts
2tbsps very low-fat fromage frais
slivers of red and yellow pepper

Briefly fry the mushrooms and garlic in the olive oil in a large frying pan. Add the white wine and simmer until the mushrooms are cooked and the cooking liquid has been absorbed. Place the mixture in a food processor with the almonds or hazelnuts and blend into a coarse paste. Fold in the fromage frais and chill before serving, garnished with thin slices of red and yellow pepper.

Bean and aubergine pâté: *Serves 4*

 1 medium aubergine
 2 garlic cloves
 400g (14oz) can butter beans, drained
 45ml (3tbsps) live natural yoghurt
 juice and grated rind of ¹/₂ lemon
 3tbsps chopped fresh herbs
 ¹/₄ tsp cumin
 ¹/₄ tsp coriander
 30ml (2tbsps) olive oil

Halve the aubergine, prick with a fork and cook with the whole garlic cloves (unpeeled) in the microwave on full power for 5-6 minutes or until soft, or in the oven at 200°C (400°F, gas mark 6) for 30 minutes. Cool and scoop out the flesh and peel the garlic, place these in a blender or food processor together with the beans, yoghurt, lemon, herbs and spices and blend to a smooth purée, dribble in the oil and mix to incorporate. Taste and adjust seasoning and flavourings if necessary.

Houmous: Serve as the traditional Greek dip, or as a delicious filling for sandwiches or baked potatoes. *Serves 2–4*

 50g (2oz) cooked chick peas (see page 64)
 juice of 1 lemon
 2 cloves garlic, crushed
 1tbsp olive oil
 1tbsp tahini
 50ml (2fl oz) water (optional)
 1tbsp freshly chopped parsley
 1tbsp pine nuts

Place all the ingredients apart from the parsley and pine nuts in a food processor and blend until smooth. Add a little water if necessary to achieve the required consistency. Serve garnished with parsley and pine nuts.

Tapenade: This rich olive paste comes from Provence and is delicious on small chunks of rye bread. Wonderfully easy to make requiring no cooking, it can also be served hot with a mixture of rices and green beans, or used to coat cubes of tofu. *Makes 175g (6oz)*

>   100g (4oz) pitted black olives, chopped
>   2tbsps capers, rinsed in milk to remove excess salt
>   2 cloves garlic, crushed
>   3tbsps olive oil or hazelnut oil
>   freshly ground black pepper
>   chopped fresh oregano or basil or thyme to taste

Quite simply, blend all the ingredients except the herbs together in a food processor or pass them through a sieve to form a smooth paste. Garnish with oregano, basil or thyme and serve.

SALADS

Pasta and Puy lentil salad: This salad is both filling and high in protein. Brown or red lentils may be used, but the black Puy variety have an especially nutty flavour and tend to retain their shape better when cooked. *Serves 4–6 as a side salad*

>   100g (4oz) Puy lentils, rinsed
>   100g (4oz) wholewheat pasta shapes
>   450g (1lb) cherry tomatoes, halved for the dressing
>   30ml (2tbsps) good quality wine vinegar
>   45ml (2tbsps) olive oil
>   4tbsps fresh parsley, finely chopped
>   2tbsps fresh basil, finely chopped
>   4 spring onions, finely sliced
>   black pepper to season

Bring the lentils to the boil and simmer for 20–25 minutes. Cook the pasta in rapidly boiling water for 6–10 minutes, until just cooked. Drain both lentils and pasta and mix together in a large bowl. Add the tomatoes. Mix all the dressing ingredients together either by whisking in a jug or shaking in a large screw-top jar. Pour over the salad and stir to coat the pasta, lentils and tomatoes.

Pasta sunshine salad: *Serves 4*
>   *100g (4oz) wholewheat pasta shapes*
>   *2 carrots, coarsely grated*
>   *1 large apple, chopped*
>   *1 orange, cut into segments*
>   *1 head of chicory, sliced*
>   *2 celery stalks, sliced*
>   *fresh parsley, chopped*
>   *2tbsps walnuts, hazelnuts or pine nuts*
>   For the dressing:
>   *5ml (1tsp) smooth mild mustard*
>   *15ml (1tbsp) red wine vinegar*
>   *60ml (4tbsps) tomato juice*
>   *freshly ground black pepper*
>   *15-30ml (1-2tbsps) walnut or hazelnut oil*

Cook the pasta until still firm, drain and rinse with cold water. When completely cooled, add the grated carrot, apple, orange, chicory, celery and parsley. Mix all the ingredients for the low-calorie tomato dressing together and pour over the salad. Toss well and serve on a bed of salad greens, watercress or alfalfa sprouts and garnish with nuts.

Warm goat's cheese salad: Goat's cheese is more easily digested than cheese made from cow's milk as its fat and protein molecules are much smaller. This is because it is intended to feed a kid which, unlike a calf, is similar in size to a human baby. *Serves 4*

175g (6oz) goat's cheese
1tbsp olive oil
16 mixed salad leaves
50g (2oz) sunflower seeds
For the dressing:
1tbsp safflower oil or olive oil
2tsps lemon juice
freshly ground black pepper
1/4 tsp mustard
pinch freshly grated root ginger
1/2 clove garlic, crushed

Preheat the grill or the oven to 180°C (350°F, gas mark 4). Slice the goat's cheese into four thick slices. Brush a baking tray with the olive oil and place the cheese slices on it. Heat in the oven or under a medium grill until melted and lightly browned. Meanwhile, toss the salad leaves in the dressing and arrange on four small plates. Place one slice of goat's cheese in the centre. Sprinkle with sunflower seeds and serve immediately.

Sunshine salad: This salad makes an attractive starter or light lunch dish. You can adapt the recipe according to the salad leaves and fresh herbs available. Sun-dried tomatoes (in bottles) are available from larger delicatessens and Italian food shops. *Serves 6*

4 large carrots, grated
225g (8oz) mixed salad leaves, such as spinach, radiccio, frisée,
  oakleaf and batavia lettuces, endive and lamb's lettuce
50g (2oz) mixed herb leaves, such as chervil, basil and roquette
50g (2oz) sun-dried tomatoes, finely chopped
50g (2oz) hazelnuts, almonds or pecans, finely chopped
For the dressing:
150ml (1/4 pint) olive oil
25ml (1fl oz) fresh lime juice
2tsps French mustard
freshly ground black pepper

Mix together the dressing ingredients. Pour half the dressing over the grated carrots. Put the carrots in the centre of a large, flat serving platter. Arrange the mixed salad and herb leaves round the outside. Sprinkle with the chopped, sun-dried tomatoes and nuts. Pour on the remaining salad dressing and serve immediately.

MAIN COURSES
Pumpkin pilaff: *Serves 2*

> *175g (6oz) long-grain rice (or a mixture of long-grain and wild rice)*
> *4tbsps olive oil*
> *1 onion, chopped*
> *6–8 no-soak apricots, thinly sliced*
> *450g (1lb) peeled pumpkin, de-seeded*
> *1 green pepper, de-seeded*
> *50g (2oz) soft brown sugar*
> *100g (4oz) pumpkin seeds*

Preheat the oven to 180°C (350°F, gas mark 4). Heat 1tbsp of the oil in a deep saucepan, add the onion and fry for 5 minutes or until translucent. Rinse the rice thoroughly and add to the onion. Stir until all the rice is coated with oil, then add twice the volume of water as there is rice. Bring to the boil, then reduce the heat and simmer for 10 minutes. Add the apricots and cook for a further 5 minutes. Drain the rice and rinse under cold running water. Slice the pumpkin and the green pepper into bite-sized chunks. Add half the pumpkin and all the pepper to the rice mixture, together with half the sugar, 1tbsp of the remaining olive oil and the pumpkin seeds. Place in a greased ovenproof dish and arrange the remaining pumpkin over the top. Brush with the remaining oil and sprinkle over the rest of the sugar. Cover and bake for 40–45 minutes.

Risotto primavera: This excellent risotto dish was devised by my husband Paddy, and has become a firm family favourite. Any leftovers may be kept in the fridge for 2–3 days, or frozen for future use. *Serves 4*

> 3 medium-sized carrots, finely chopped
> 1 medium onion, finely chopped
> 6tbsps olive oil
> 250g (9oz) Arborio rice
> 1 large courgette, finely chopped
> 1.2 litres (2 pints) vegetable stock (see page 67)
> 8 fresh basil leaves
> 1tsp balsamic vinegar
> 4tbsps Parmesan cheese, finely grated

Place half the quantity of chopped carrot together with the chopped onion in the olive oil and lightly fry for 2-3 minutes. Stir in the arborio rice until it is coated with the oil. Add the courgette pieces and slowly add the vegetable stock, stirring continuously. Chop the basil leaves and add to the mixture. Add the remaining half of the chopped carrots. Continue to stir in the vegetable stock until the rice has cooked through (approximately 25 minutes in total). Stir in the balsamic vinegar and sprinkle over the Parmesan cheese to taste. Serve immediately. *Note:* Arborio rice is the best type to use for this recipe as it gives a deliciously creamy result. Arborio rice can be found in Italian delicatessens and specialist shops.

Buckwheat bonanza: This buckwheat feast works well with the stronger flavours of wild mushrooms such as the shiitake or oyster varieties. If you have the time, fresh artichoke hearts are the tastiest, otherwise, tinned artichoke hearts can be used. *Serves 2*

> 50g (2oz) roasted buckwheat (kasha)
> 50g (2oz) buckwheat
> 450ml (¾ pint) water
> 100g (4oz) artichoke hearts

1tbsp olive oil
100g (4oz) button or fresh wild mushrooms, roughly chopped
4 spring onions, chopped
1tsp dried sage and parsley or 2tsps fresh sage and parsley
1tsp tamari sauce
freshly ground black pepper
25g (1oz) pecan nuts (optional)

Rinse the buckwheat in a sieve under a running tap. Bring the water to the boil, add the buckwheat, cover and simmer for 15 minutes or until soft. Meanwhile, if using fresh artichokes, trim and cook them in minimal water or in a steamer. When soft, remove the leaves and trim away the toughened fibres to reveal the soft hearts. If using tinned artichoke hearts these will be precooked. Roughly chop the artichokes. In a large frying pan heat the oil and gently soften the mushrooms and spring onions. Drain and add the buckwheat, chopped artichokes and herbs, and stir well. Add the tamari sauce, and freshly ground black pepper to season. Serve sprinkled with pecan nuts, if using.

Millet croquettes: Both children and adults love these. Serve them warm with a tomato sauce (made simply by cooking and puréeing fresh tomatoes). Cooked brown rice may be substituted for the millet. *Makes 18*

450g (1lb) cooked millet
1 onion, peeled and finely chopped
100g (4oz) green vegetables (eg broccoli or beans or cour-
gettes), chopped
2tbsps tamari sauce
50g (2oz) wholewheat plain flour
150ml (¼ pint) water or vegetable stock (optional)
1tsp olive oil

Preheat the oven to 200°C (400°F, gas mark 6). Mix all the ingredients except the water or stock together in a large bowl and knead for 5–10 minutes. If the dough seems too loose, add additional flour. Roll the mixture into small balls and press flat. Lay the croquettes on a lightly oiled baking sheet and bake for 20 minutes.

No-cook rissoles: *Makes 8 small rissoles*
    175g (6oz) mixed nuts (eg hazelnuts and almonds), ground
    100g (4oz) wholewheat breadcrumbs
    1/2 tbsp finely chopped onion
    1tbsp chopped parsley
    1tsp low-salt yeast extract blended with 1tbsp water
    1/2 tbsp poppy or sesame seeds
Reserve about one-quarter of the nuts and breadcrumbs for coating, and mix all the remaining ingredients together. Form into small rissoles. Mix together the reserved nuts and breadcrumbs and use to coat the rissoles. Serve with a herb salad.

Quick pasta sauces:
Use these sauces to transform fresh or dried pasta into a culinary extravaganza. Simply blend the ingredients together in a bowl before mixing into cooked, drained pasta. These three easy pasta recipes are delicious served with vegetables, chicken or fish dishes, or served on their own as a starter. The sauces can also be used to liven up plain baked potatoes.
Tomato and herb:
    30ml (2tbsps) olive oil
    15ml (1tbsp) cider vinegar
    15ml (1tbsp) tomato purée
    5ml (1tsp) garlic purée, optional
    1tsp dried oregano or 1tbsp fresh chopped herbs
Parmesan, garlic and herb:
    30ml (2tbsps) olive or sunflower oil
    50g (2oz) freshly grated Parmesan cheese
    2 cloves garlic, crushed
    25g (1oz) freshly chopped herbs

Lemon and olive:
>   *30ml (2tbsps) virgin olive or walnut oil*
>   *freshly grated zest from 1 lemon*
>   *15ml (1tbsp) lemon juice*
>   *25g (1oz) fresh chopped parsley*
>   *50g (2oz) black olives, quartered*

Tofu and onion flan: A delicious dairy and gluten-free flan made with buckwheat pastry. Serve hot with baked beetroot and steamed broccoli. *Serves 4*

>   For the pastry:
>   *100g (4oz) buckwheat flour*
>   *25g (1oz) poppy seeds*
>   *2tbsps walnut or hazelnut oil*
>   *50ml (2fl oz) ice-cold water*
>   For the filling:
>   *1tsp olive oil*
>   *225g (8oz) red onions, peeled and finely sliced*
>   *225g (8oz) white onions, peeled and finely sliced*
>   *225g (8oz) silken tofu*
>   *150ml (1/4 pint) soya milk*
>   *2tsps mustard*
>   *freshly ground black pepper*
>   *2 free-range eggs, size 3*

Preheat the oven to 200°C (400°F, gas mark 6). Mix the flour and poppy seeds in a food processor, and slowly dribble in the oil. Add only enough of the water to enable the dough to form a ball round the blade. Put the dough in a bowl, cover with a cloth and place in the fridge for 30 minutes. Meanwhile fry the onions in the olive oil until transparent. Place the tofu in the food processor and blend until smooth and the consistency of double cream. Add the other ingredients and blend again.

Roll out the pastry and use to line a 20cm (8 inch) flan dish. Bake blind for 10 minutes, and take out the pastry. Reduce the oven temperature to 160°C (325°F, gas mark 3). Arrange the onions in the pastry case and pour over the tofu mixture. Bake for 45 minutes or until set and turning golden brown.

Vegetables with dhal sauce: *Serves 4*

>   *225g (8oz) red lentils*
>   *600ml (1 pint) vegetable stock (see page 67) or water*
>   *30ml (2tbsps) olive oil or sesame oil*
>   *1 onion, chopped*
>   *1 garlic clove, crushed*
>   *1 scant tbsp freshly grated ginger*
>   *1/2 tsp turmeric*
>   *1 tsp coriander*
>   *freshly grated black pepper*

Place the lentils in a saucepan with the stock, oil, onion, garlic, ginger, spices and pepper, bring to the boil, cover and reduce the heat to a very slow simmer. Cook for about 30 minutes, stirring occasionally and adding more stock if necessary to give a soft but not too thick sauce. Serve with steamed vegetables and wholegrain rice.

Marinated tofu with vegetables and noodles: *Serves 4*

>   *225g (8oz) firm tofu*
>   *30ml (2tbsps) light soy sauce*
>   *30ml (2tbsps) clear honey*
>   *2 1/2 ml (1/2 level tsp) Chinese five-spice powder or allspice*
>   *30ml (2tbsps) unrefined sesame or sunflower oil*
>   *1 red pepper, sliced*
>   *1 yellow pepper, sliced*
>   *100g (4oz) mange-tout, green beans or broccoli*
>   *100g (4oz) baby sweetcorn, fennel or asparagus*
>   *225g (8oz) egg noodles*
>   *15ml (1 level tbsp) toasted sesame seeds*

Cut the tofu into thick slices and halve each slice. Mix together the soy sauce, honey, spice and half the oil and pour the marinade over the tofu, cover and leave for at least an hour. Steam or stir-fry the vegetables until just tender and cook the egg noodles. Meanwhile heat the remaining oil and sauté the tofu for 1/2 minute on each side. Serve the tofu arranged over the egg noodles and vegetables. Sprinkle with toasted sesame seeds.

Broccoli and pine nut stir-fry: A stir-fry makes a quick and tasty lunch or light supper dish. The high heat generated in the wok or large frying pan cooks the vegetables quickly and preserves their vitamin content. *Serves 2–3 as a main course*

　　10ml (2tsps) olive oil
　　50g (2oz) pine nuts
　　15g (1tbsp) sun-dried tomatoes, chopped
　　350g (12oz) broccoli florets
　　350g (12oz) Chinese leaves, chopped
　　15ml (1tbsp) dry sherry or mirin (from health shops)
　　juice of 1 lemon
　　15ml (1tbsp) water
　　black pepper to season

Heat the wok or large frying pan. Add the oil and lightly fry the pine nuts. Remove from the oil and drain on kitchen paper. Add the vegetables and fry for 3–4 minutes, stirring all the time. Pour over the liquids and add the seasoning. Stir well. Sprinkle over the toasted pine nuts and serve immediately.

Bean and leek bake: *Serves 4*

　　450g (1lb) leeks
　　400g (14oz) can butter beans, or fresh broad beans
　　25ml (1 1/2 tbsps) safflower oil or olive oil
　　25ml (1 1/2 level tbsps) plain flour
　　150ml (1/4 pint) semi-skimmed milk or soya milk
　　700g (1 1/2 lb) potatoes, thinly sliced

Preheat the oven to 200°C (400°F, gas mark 6). Trim and slice the leeks and cook in a little water until just tender, drain and reserve about 150ml (¼ pint) of the cooking liquid. Heat the oil in a small non-stick saucepan, add the flour and cook together for one minute, add the milk and reserved vegetable stock and bring to the boil, stirring together to form a smooth sauce. Place the cooked leeks and drained beans into the base of an oven-proof dish, pour over the sauce. Arrange the sliced potatoes over the top, overlapping the layers. Brush with a little extra oil and bake in the oven, for 35–40 minutes or until tender and golden brown.

Tofu stuffed tomatoes: Tofu is a high-protein ingredient that makes a good pâté or stuffing. This mixture can also be used as as filling for savoury tarts. *Serves 6 as a cold starter*

> *100g (4oz) sunflower seeds*
> *25g (1oz) sesame seeds*
> *175g (10oz) silken tofu*
> *15ml (1tbsp) sunflower or sesame oil*
> *100g (4oz) grated carrot*
> *½ tsp paprika*
> *black pepper to season*
> *6 large tomatoes*

Use a coffee grinder or food processor to grind the seeds to a fine powder. Mix in a bowl with the tofu and oil, stir thoroughly until smooth. Add the grated carrot and seasonings, mix well. Use a sharp knife to slice the top off each tomato and a teaspoon to scoop out the seeds. Stuff with the tofu mixture, replace the tomato tops and serve.

IDEAS FOR ENTERTAINING

Wild mushroom and walnut roast: The best nut roasts are full of flavour and moist in texture. This recipe is made with more vegetables than usual and baked in layers of contrasting tastes and textures. The filling of walnuts and wild mushrooms give this roast an especially meaty flavour. *Serves 6 as a main course*

> *30ml (2tbsps) olive oil*
> *1 large onion, finely chopped*
> *5 stalks celery, finely chopped*
> *1tbsp wholewheat flour*
> *300ml (¹/₂ pint) vegetable stock (see page 67)*
> *200g (7oz) ground almonds*
> *50g (2oz) porridge oats*
> *50g (2oz) breadcrumbs*
> *1 apple, grated*
> *juice and zest of 1 small lemon*
> *2 eggs*
> *black pepper to season*
> For the filling:
> *10ml (1tsp) olive or walnut oil*
> *1 small onion, finely chopped*
> *350g (12oz) fresh wild mushrooms (or dried mushrooms,*
>   *reconstituted)*
> *150g (5oz) walnuts, finely chopped*
> *2 cloves garlic, crushed*
> *1tbsp grated ginger root*

Preheat the oven to 190°C (375°F, gas mark 5). Fry the onion in the olive oil, and then the celery until soft. Stir in the wholewheat flour and cook for 2–3 minutes. Gradually add the vegetable stock, stirring continuously to avoid lumps. In a large bowl, mix together the ground almonds, porridge oats, breadcrumbs, grated apple, lemon juice and eggs. Stir in the hot sauce and mix well. Lightly season with pepper. To make the 'meaty' filling, fry the chopped onion in the oil. Chop the wild mushrooms and add to the onions, together with the walnuts, garlic and ginger root. Cook over a low heat for 5–10 minutes, or until the mushrooms have softened.

Lightly oil a loaf tin and line with greaseproof paper. Spoon in half of the breadcrumb mixture, layer the mushroom mix on top, then add the final layer of breadcrumb mixture. Bake in the oven for approximately 1 hour, or until the top is golden brown. Allow the tin to cool before turning out. Serve sliced with spoonfuls of tomato passata.

Asparagus and mushroom risotto: To make this tasty light supper dish even more exotic add a pinch of saffron to the cooking liquid to turn the rice yellow. Also, try mixing two types of rice (eg brown basmati and brown Italian rice) for added variety. *Serves 2*

100g (4oz) brown rice (mixed if possible), well rinsed
475ml (16fl oz) water
1 large onion, peeled and finely chopped
few strands of saffron (optional)
100g (4oz) fresh asparagus, trimmed
2tsps olive oil
100g (4oz) mushrooms, finely chopped
2tbsps chopped fresh parsley
freshly ground black pepper
juice of 1/2 lemon

Gently heat a heavy-based saucepan on top of the stove, add the rice and stir with a wooden spatula for 1 minute until lightly toasted. Add the water, onion and saffron, if using. Bring to the boil, cover and simmer for 20 minutes. Meanwhile, chop the asparagus into short lengths, reserving the tips for garnish. After the 20 minutes' cooking time add the lengths of asparagus and simmer for another 10–15 minutes until the rice is soft. In a separate pan, gently heat the olive oil and lightly sauté the asparagus tips. Remove from the pan and drain on kitchen paper. Stir the chopped mushrooms and parsley into the cooked rice mixture. Season with black pepper, stir in the lemon juice and serve garnished with the asparagus tips.

Cabbage parcels: *Serves 6*

100g (4oz) millet
450ml (15fl oz) vegetable stock (see page 67)
1 savoy cabbage
1tbsp olive oil
2 red onions, peeled and chopped
4 spring onions, sliced into rings
8 stems of fresh coriander
2 cloves garlic, crushed
3 carrots, chopped
2 leeks, chopped
4 tomatoes, chopped
100g (4oz) okra, chopped
juice of 1 lime
freshly ground black pepper
2tbsps water or stock

Preheat the oven to 180°C (350°F, gas mark 4). Place the millet and stock in a saucepan, bring to the boil, cover and simmer for about 20 minutes or until the millet is soft. Separate the cabbage into whole leaves and blanch them in boiling water for 30 seconds. Set aside to drain on kitchen paper. Chop the stems of the coriander. Chop the leaves and set on one side. Heat the oil and gently fry the onion, coriander stems and garlic until the onion is transparent. Add the chopped carrots and leeks and continue to cook for another minute. Add the tomatoes, okra, the chopped coriander leaves and stir in the cooked millet. Add the lime juice, and freshly ground black pepper to season.

Place a dessertspoonful of the millet mixture on a cabbage leaf and roll up, folding in the sides as you go. Repeat until all the cabbage leaves have been filled. Place in an ovenproof dish, spoon over the 2tbsps of water or stock, cover and bake for 20 minutes.

Five-vegetable terrine: This multi-coloured terrine may be served hot or cold. For an attractive starter, slice and serve it in the centre of a plate of freshly squeezed (or bottled) tomato juice. *Serves 6–8*

450g (1lb) carrots, cubed
225g (8oz) celeriac, cubed
350g (12oz) fresh spinach
350g (12oz) broccoli, in florets
225g (8oz) leeks, white part only, sliced
freshly ground black pepper
juice of 1 orange
6 free-range eggs, size 3

Preheat the oven to 200°C (400°F, gas mark 6). Cook the carrots and celeriac in boiling water in separate saucepans until tender. Cook the spinach in a little water for about 5–6 minutes. Blanch the broccoli and leeks in boiling water, separately, for 1–2 minutes. Drain all the vegetables well.

In a food processor, blend the leek and celeriac with a pinch of black pepper and two eggs until puréed to a coarse texture. Repeat, using the broccoli, spinach and two of the eggs. Finally, repeat the process with the carrot, adding the orange juice and the two remaining eggs.

Line a 1kg (2lb) loaf tin with lightly oiled baking parchment or greaseproof paper. Spread the green spinach and broccoli mixture over the bottom and follow with a cream-coloured layer of leek and celeriac. Finally, top with a layer of carrot and orange purée. Place the loaf tin inside a large roasting tin filled with about 1cm (½ inch) of hot water. Bake for about 1 hour or until set. Turn out on a serving dish, allow to cool slightly then peel off the baking parchment before slicing the terrine.

Useful Addresses

British Dietetic Association
7th Floor, Elizabeth House
22 Suffolk Street
Queensway
Birmingham
West Midlands B1 1LS
Telephone: 021 643 5483

British Nutrition Foundation
High Holborn House
52-54 High Holborn
London WC1V 6RQ
Telephone: 071 404 6504

British Union for Abolition of
Vivisection (BUAV)
16A Crane Grove
London N7 8LB
Telephone: 071 700 4888

The Coeliac Society
PO Box 220
High Wycombe
Buckinghamshire HP11 2HY

Consumers' Association
2 Marylebone Road
London NW1 4DF
Telephone: 071 486 5544

Food and Drink Association
6 Catherine Street
London WC2B 5JJ
Telephone: 071 836 2460

The Food Commission
3rd Floor,
5-11 Worship Street
London EC2A 2BH
Telephone: 071 628 7774

Health Education Authority
Hamilton House
Mabledon Place
London WC1H 9TX
Telephone: 071 383 3833

Vegetarian Society of the
United Kingdom
Parkdale
Dunham Road
Altrincham
Cheshire WA14 4QG
Telephone: 061 928 0793

Index

HOW TO ORDER YOUR BOXTREE BOOKS BY LIZ EARLE

LIZ EARLE'S QUICK GUIDES

Available Now

☐	1 85283 542 7	Aromatherapy	£3.99
☐	1 85283 544 3	Baby and Toddler Foods	£3.99
☐	1 85283 543 5	Food Facts	£3.99
☐	1 85283 546 X	Vegetarian Cookery	£3.99

Available from September 1994

☐	0 7522 1619 8	Evening Primrose Oil	£3.99
☐	0 7522 1614 7	Herbs for Health	£3.99
☐	1 85283 984 8	Successful Slimming	£3.99
☐	1 85283 989 9	Vitamins and Minerals	£3.99

ACE PLAN TITLES

☐	1 85283 518 4	Liz Earle's Ace Plan The New Guide to Super Vitamins A, C and E	£4.99
☐	1 85283 554 0	Liz Earle's Ace Plan Weight-Loss for Life	£4.99

All these books are available at your local bookshop or can be ordered direct from the publisher. Just tick the titles you want and fill in the form below.

Prices and availability subject to change without notice.

Boxtree Cash Sales, P O Box 11, Falmouth, Cornwall TR10 9EN

Please send cheque or postal order for the value of the book, and add the following for postage and packing:

UK including BFPO – £1.00 for one book, plus 50p for the second book, and 30p for each additional book ordered up to a £3.00 maximum.

OVERSEAS including Eire – £2.00 for the first book, plus £1.00 for the second book, and 50p for each additional book ordered.

OR please debit this amount from my Access/Visa Card (delete as appropriate).

Card Number ☐☐☐☐☐☐☐☐☐☐☐☐☐☐☐☐☐☐☐

AMOUNT £ ....

EXPIRY DATE ....

SIGNED ....

NAME ....

ADDRESS ....

....